© 2024 by FAISAL JAMIL. All rights reserved.

Title: "Mastering Complex Problem Solving: A Comprehensive Guide"

This book, along with its contents encompassing text, illustrations, images, diagrams, and other creative elements, is the exclusive property of FAISAL JAMIL and is safeguarded by copyright law.

FAISAL JAMIL asserts full ownership and retains all rights to this book. No part of this publication may be reproduced, distributed, or transmitted in any form or by any means, such as photocopying, recording, or electronic methods, without prior written consent from the copyright holder. Brief quotations in critical reviews and certain noncommercial uses permitted by copyright law are exceptions.

This copyright notice applies to all editions, formats, and translations of the book, whether in print, digital, or any other medium or technology existing now or developed in the future. Unauthorized use or infringement may result in legal action and pursuit of remedies under applicable copyright laws.

While efforts have been made to ensure accuracy and reliability, FAISAL JAMIL does not guarantee the completeness or suitability of the information. Readers are responsible for evaluating and using the content judiciously.

FAISAL JAMIL reserves the right to make changes, updates, or corrections to the book without prior notice. Inclusion of third-party materials or references does not imply endorsement or affiliation unless used under fair use principles or with proper permissions and attributions.

For permissions, inquiries, or requests regarding the book's use, please contact FAISAL JAMIL through official channels listed on their Amazon author page or provided email address.

This comprehensive copyright notice serves to protect FAISAL JAMIL'S intellectual property rights, maintain content control, and inform users about associated restrictions and permissions.

Warm regards,

FAISAL JAMIL

For your feedback and reviews:

http://www.amazon.com/author/faisal.jamil

Email: faisaljamilauthor@gmail.com

About the author

Certainly! Faisal Jamil is a multifaceted individual with a diverse set of skills and experiences. With a strong foundation in computer knowledge since childhood, he has developed a deep understanding of technology that informs his work as a content writer. Faisal also possesses digital skills, which further enhance his abilities in various digital platforms and technologies.

Beyond his professional endeavors, Faisal Jamil has also excelled in the martial arts, particularly Shotokan Karate, where he achieved the prestigious rank of first Dan black belt. This achievement speaks to his dedication, discipline, and commitment to personal growth and mastery.

In his professional life, Faisal Jamil has carved out a successful career in sales management within the Fast Moving Consumer Goods (FMCG) sector. His roles in various FMCG companies have honed his skills in strategic planning, team leadership, and business development. Faisal's ability to drive sales and achieve targets has been instrumental in his career progression, showcasing his talent for identifying opportunities and delivering results.

Faisal Jamil is also deeply interested in business investment strategies, planning, and execution. His understanding of these areas has been key to his success in the business world, allowing him to make informed decisions and implement effective strategies. His ability to navigate the complexities of investment planning and execution has set him apart as a strategic thinker and a valuable asset in any business endeavor.

Overall, Faisal Jamil is a dynamic individual who combines his passion for technology, martial arts, sales management, digital skills, and business investment strategies to achieve success in diverse fields. His journey is a testament to his versatility, resilience, and continuous pursuit of excellence.

Yours Sincerely

FAISAL JAMIL

For your feedback and reviews:

https://www.amazon.com/author/faisal.jamil

Email: faisaljamilauthor@gmail.com

MASTERING COMPLEX PROBLEM SOLVING

A COMPREHENSIVE GUIDE

Table of Content

Preface

Introduction

Chapter 1: Understanding the Nature of Complex Problems

Chapter 2: Developing a Problem-Solving Mindset

Chapter 3: Enhancing Analytical Thinking Skills

Chapter 4: Embracing Systems Thinking

Chapter 5: Harnessing Creativity and Innovation

Chapter 6: Utilizing Problem-Solving Tools and Techniques

Chapter 7: Making Decisions Under Uncertainty

Chapter 8: Effective Communication in Problem Solving

Chapter 9: Collaborative Problem Solving

Chapter 10: Ethical Considerations in Complex Problem Solving

Chapter 11: Implementing Solutions and Monitoring Progress

Chapter 12: Learning from Failure and Iterating Solutions

Chapter 13: Building Resilience in Problem Solving

Chapter 14: Applying Problem-Solving Skills in Different Contexts

Chapter 15: Leveraging Technology in Problem Solving

Chapter 16: Future Trends in Complex Problem Solving

Chapter 17: Case Studies in Complex Problem Solving

Chapter 18: Cultivating a Culture of Continuous Learning

Chapter 19: The Role of Leadership in Complex Problem Solving

Chapter 20: Conclusion: Becoming a Master Problem Solver

Preface

Welcome to "Mastering Complex Problem Solving: A Comprehensive Guide." This book is designed to be your go-to resource for developing the skills and mindset needed to tackle the most challenging problems you may encounter in your personal and professional life.

Problem-solving is a fundamental skill that we use every day, whether we are aware of it or not. From solving a crossword puzzle to resolving a conflict at work, our ability to solve problems directly impacts our success and satisfaction in life. However, as problems become more complex, the strategies and approaches we use must also evolve.

This book is divided into several chapters, each focusing on a different aspect of complex problem-solving. We start by defining what complex problems are and discussing their characteristics. We then explore various types of complex problems and the importance of identifying them early.

Next, we delve into the mindset needed for effective problem-solving, including cultivating curiosity, embracing ambiguity, and overcoming mental blocks. We also discuss the importance of breaking down problems into manageable parts, identifying patterns and trends, and utilizing data and evidence effectively.

Communication and collaboration are key components of problem-solving, so we provide guidance on how to communicate ideas clearly, listen actively, and collaborate effectively. We also explore the role of leadership in problem-solving and how leaders can lead by example to foster a culture of innovation.

Throughout the book, we provide practical tips, tools, and techniques that you can apply to your own problem-solving efforts. Whether you are facing a complex business challenge or a personal dilemma, this book will provide you with the strategies and insights you need to find creative and effective solutions.

We hope that "Mastering Complex Problem Solving: A Comprehensive Guide" will become your go-to resource for tackling the most challenging problems with confidence and clarity. By developing your problem-solving skills, you can become a more effective leader, a more valuable team member, and a more successful individual.

Introduction

In today's fast-paced and ever-changing world, the ability to solve complex problems is more important than ever. Whether you're a business leader, a team manager, or an individual contributor, the ability to tackle complex challenges with confidence and clarity can set you apart from the competition.

"Mastering Complex Problem Solving: A Comprehensive Guide" is designed to help you develop the skills and mindset needed to excel in problem-solving. This book is not just about finding solutions to problems; it's about understanding the nature of complex problems, developing a structured approach to solving them, and continuously learning and adapting to new challenges.

In this introduction, we'll provide an overview of what you can expect from this book and why mastering complex problem-solving is essential in today's world.

1: Understanding Complex Problems

We'll start by defining what complex problems are and discussing their characteristics. You'll learn why traditional problem-solving approaches may not be effective for complex problems and why a new approach is needed.

2: Types of Complex Problems

Next, we'll explore various types of complex problems, from technical challenges to organizational issues. You'll learn how to identify different types of complex problems and tailor your approach accordingly.

3: Developing the Right Mindset

Effective problem-solving starts with the right mindset. We'll discuss the importance of curiosity, open-mindedness, and resilience in tackling complex problems.

4: Tools and Techniques

We'll introduce you to a variety of tools and techniques that can help you analyze complex problems, generate innovative solutions, and make informed decisions.

5: Communication and Collaboration

Problem-solving is often a team effort. We'll provide guidance on how to communicate your ideas clearly, listen actively to others, and collaborate effectively to find solutions.

6: Leadership in Problem-Solving

Finally, we'll discuss the role of leadership in problem-solving and how leaders can create a culture that fosters innovation and creativity.

By the end of this book, you'll have the knowledge, skills, and mindset needed to tackle even the most challenging problems with confidence and clarity. Whether you're facing a complex business challenge, a personal dilemma, or a global crisis, "Mastering Complex Problem Solving: A Comprehensive Guide" will be your go-to resource for finding innovative solutions.

Chapter 1

Understanding the Nature of Complex Problems

A: Definition and Characteristics of Complex Problems

Definition

Complex problems are issues or challenges that are intricate, multifaceted, and often do not have straightforward solutions. They typically involve multiple factors and stakeholders, making them difficult to analyze and solve using traditional problem-solving approaches.

Characteristics of Complex Problems

1: Multiple Interconnected Elements

Complex problems are composed of various interconnected elements that influence each other. Changes in one element can lead to unpredictable effects on others.

2: Uncertainty and Ambiguity

Complex problems are often characterized by uncertainty and ambiguity. Key information may be missing or incomplete, making it challenging to understand the full scope of the problem.

3: Dynamic and Evolving Nature

Complex problems are dynamic and evolve over time. Factors contributing to the problem may change, requiring continuous monitoring and adaptation of solutions.

4: Conflicting Stakeholder Interests

Complex problems often involve stakeholders with conflicting interests. Balancing these interests to find a solution that satisfies all parties can be a significant challenge.

5: Nonlinear Relationships

Complex problems often exhibit nonlinear relationships, meaning that small changes can lead to disproportionately large effects, or that effects may not be proportional to causes.

6: Emergent Properties

Complex systems can exhibit emergent properties, where the whole system behaves in ways that cannot be predicted by analyzing the individual parts. This makes predicting outcomes challenging.

7: Wickedness

Complex problems are sometimes referred to as "wicked problems" due to their elusive nature. They may not have a definitive solution and may require ongoing management rather than a one-time fix.

8: Highly Context-Dependent

Solutions to complex problems are often highly dependent on the specific context in which the problem arises. What works in one situation may not work in another.

Example

An example of a complex problem is climate change. Climate change involves a multitude of interconnected factors, including greenhouse gas emissions, deforestation, and industrial practices. The effects of climate change, such as rising sea levels and extreme weather events, are dynamic and can vary depending on the region. Additionally, addressing climate change requires balancing the interests of various stakeholders, including governments, industries, and environmental groups, who may have conflicting priorities. The nonlinear nature of climate change means that small reductions in greenhouse gas emissions may not have a proportional impact on mitigating its effects, requiring comprehensive and coordinated efforts to address the problem.

B: Types of Complex Problems

Complex problems can manifest in various forms across different domains. Understanding the types of complex problems can help in developing specific strategies for solving them. Here are some common types:

1: Dynamic Problems

These problems involve elements that change over time, leading to evolving challenges. Examples include economic fluctuations, climate change, and market trends. Solutions for dynamic problems often require continuous adaptation and monitoring.

2: Interconnected Problems

Interconnected problems are characterized by multiple elements or components that are interdependent. Changes in one element can have ripple effects on others. Examples include ecosystem dynamics and supply chain disruptions. Solving interconnected problems requires understanding and managing these interdependencies.

3: Wicked Problems

Wicked problems are complex issues that are difficult to define and have no clear solution. They often involve conflicting values, incomplete information, and changing requirements. Examples include poverty, healthcare access, and climate change. Wicked problems require innovative and adaptive approaches due to their elusive nature.

4: Chaotic Problems

Chaotic problems are characterized by high levels of uncertainty and rapid change. They often occur during crises or emergencies, such as natural disasters or pandemics. Solutions for chaotic problems require quick decision-making and flexibility in response to changing circumstances.

5: Comprehensive Problems

Comprehensive problems are broad in scope and involve multiple dimensions. They require holistic approaches that consider various factors and perspectives. Examples include urban planning and sustainable development. Solutions for comprehensive problems require interdisciplinary collaboration and long-term planning.

6: Social Complexity

Socially complex problems involve human behavior and societal structures. They often involve multiple stakeholders with diverse interests and values. Examples include social inequality, political conflicts, and cultural issues. Solutions for socially complex problems require understanding human behavior and addressing underlying societal issues.

7: Technical Complexity

Technical complex problems involve intricate systems or technologies. They often require specialized knowledge and expertise to understand and solve. Examples include advanced engineering projects and technological innovations. Solutions for technical complex problems require advanced technical skills and innovative approaches.

Understanding the different types of complex problems can help individuals and organizations approach them more effectively. By identifying the specific characteristics of a complex problem, stakeholders can develop tailored strategies and solutions to address them.

C: The Importance of Identifying Complex Problems Early

Identifying complex problems early in their development is crucial for several reasons. Early detection allows for timely intervention and mitigation, potentially preventing the problem from escalating into a larger issue. Here are some key reasons why identifying complex problems early is important:

1: Prevention of Escalation

Complex problems often start as minor issues or anomalies that, if left unaddressed, can grow in scale and complexity. By identifying these problems early, organizations can take proactive measures to prevent them from escalating into more significant challenges.

2: Cost Savings

Addressing complex problems early can result in cost savings. Early intervention is often less resource-intensive than dealing with a problem after it has grown in complexity. By identifying and addressing problems early, organizations can avoid costly disruptions and damage control efforts.

3: Maintaining Reputation and Trust

Complex problems, if not managed effectively, can damage an organization's reputation and erode trust among stakeholders. Early identification and effective management of problems demonstrate proactive and responsible behavior, helping to maintain trust and credibility.

4: Improved Decision Making

Early identification of complex problems provides organizations with more time to gather information, analyze the situation, and make informed decisions. This can lead to more effective problem-solving strategies and better outcomes.

5: Opportunity for Innovation

Early identification of complex problems can also create opportunities for innovation. By addressing problems early, organizations can explore new approaches and technologies that may not have been considered if the problem had been allowed to escalate.

6: Enhanced Organizational Resilience

Organizations that are adept at identifying and addressing complex problems early are more resilient. They can quickly adapt to changing circumstances and mitigate the impact of problems on their operations.

7: Improved Stakeholder Relations

Early identification and effective management of complex problems can enhance stakeholder relations. By keeping stakeholders informed and involved in the problem-solving process, organizations can build trust and collaboration.

In conclusion, identifying complex problems early is essential for organizations seeking to proactively manage risks, maintain operational efficiency, and preserve their reputation. Early detection enables organizations to take timely and effective action, leading to better outcomes and enhanced organizational resilience.

Chapter 2
Developing a Problem-Solving Mindset

A: Cultivating Curiosity and Open-Mindedness

Cultivating curiosity and open-mindedness is essential for effective problem-solving, especially when dealing with complex issues. These qualities help individuals approach problems with a fresh perspective, explore innovative solutions, and remain flexible in the face of uncertainty. Here's a detailed look at how curiosity and open-mindedness contribute to problem-solving:

1: Curiosity as a Driving Force

Curiosity is the desire to seek new information, experiences, and knowledge. It drives individuals to ask questions, explore new possibilities, and challenge assumptions. In problem-solving, curiosity encourages individuals to dig deeper, uncover root causes, and consider alternative perspectives.

2: Open-Mindedness and Acceptance of New Ideas

Open-mindedness is the willingness to consider new ideas, perspectives, and information. It involves setting aside preconceived notions and being receptive to different viewpoints. Open-minded individuals are more likely to explore unconventional solutions and collaborate effectively with others.

3: Enhanced Creativity and Innovation

Curiosity and open-mindedness are closely linked to creativity and innovation. By fostering a curious mindset, individuals can generate new ideas, think outside the box, and approach problems from different angles. Open-mindedness allows for the integration of diverse perspectives and ideas, leading to innovative solutions.

4: Improved Problem Framing

Curiosity and open-mindedness help individuals frame problems in a more comprehensive and insightful manner. By questioning assumptions and exploring various facets of a problem, individuals can gain a deeper understanding of its complexity and identify novel approaches to solving it.

5: Adaptability and Flexibility

Complex problems often require adaptability and flexibility in problem-solving approaches. Curiosity and open-mindedness enable individuals to adapt to changing circumstances, consider alternative solutions, and pivot when necessary.

6: Resilience in the Face of Failure

Curiosity and open-mindedness can also help individuals bounce back from failure. Instead of viewing failure as a setback, curious individuals see it as an opportunity to learn and improve. Open-mindedness allows for the exploration of new strategies and approaches after experiencing failure.

7: Continuous Learning and Growth

Cultivating curiosity and open-mindedness fosters a mindset of continuous learning and growth. Individuals who are curious and open-minded are more likely to seek out new knowledge, skills, and experiences, which can enhance their problem-solving abilities over time.

In conclusion, cultivating curiosity and open-mindedness is essential for effective problem-solving, particularly in dealing with complex issues. These qualities not only lead to more innovative and creative solutions but also foster a mindset of continuous learning and adaptation, which is crucial in today's rapidly changing world.

B: Embracing Ambiguity and Uncertainty

Embracing ambiguity and uncertainty is a critical aspect of effective problem-solving, especially in complex situations where outcomes are unpredictable. Rather than viewing ambiguity and uncertainty as obstacles, individuals who embrace them see them as opportunities for growth, innovation, and creative thinking. Here's a detailed exploration of how embracing ambiguity and uncertainty contributes to problem-solving:

1: Increased Adaptability

Embracing ambiguity and uncertainty allows individuals to adapt more easily to changing circumstances. Instead of being rigid in their thinking, they are open to new information and can adjust their approach as needed.

2: Enhanced Creativity

Ambiguity and uncertainty can stimulate creativity by encouraging individuals to think outside the box. When faced with unclear or unpredictable situations, individuals are more likely to explore unconventional ideas and solutions.

3: Improved Decision Making

Embracing ambiguity and uncertainty can lead to better decision-making. Rather than waiting for all the information to be clear, individuals can make informed decisions based on the information available, knowing that they can adjust their course if necessary.

4: Fostered Innovation

Ambiguity and uncertainty often lead to innovation. When faced with unclear problems, individuals are more likely to experiment with new approaches and technologies, leading to innovative solutions.

5: Encouraged Risk-Taking

Embracing ambiguity and uncertainty can encourage individuals to take calculated risks. When outcomes are uncertain, individuals are more willing to try new things and step outside their comfort zones.

6: Developed Resilience

Embracing ambiguity and uncertainty can help individuals develop resilience. By learning to cope with uncertainty, individuals become more adept at handling setbacks and challenges.

7: Enhanced Problem-Solving Skills

Dealing with ambiguity and uncertainty can improve problem-solving skills. Individuals learn to approach problems from different angles, consider multiple perspectives, and think critically about potential solutions.

8: Cultivated Learning Mindset

Embracing ambiguity and uncertainty fosters a mindset of continuous learning. Individuals become more curious and open-minded, seeking out new information and experiences to enhance their understanding of complex issues.

In conclusion, embracing ambiguity and uncertainty is essential for effective problem-solving, particularly in complex situations. By viewing ambiguity and uncertainty as opportunities rather than obstacles, individuals can enhance their adaptability, creativity, and resilience, leading to more innovative and effective solutions.

C: Overcoming Mental Blocks and Biases

Overcoming mental blocks and biases is crucial for effective problem-solving, especially in complex situations where clear thinking and objective analysis are essential. Mental blocks and biases can cloud judgment, limit creativity, and hinder decision-making. Here's a detailed exploration of how overcoming mental blocks and biases contributes to problem-solving:

1: Awareness of Biases

The first step in overcoming biases is to be aware of them. Recognizing common biases such as confirmation bias (favoring information that confirms preconceptions) or anchoring bias (relying too heavily on the first piece of information encountered) can help individuals avoid falling into these traps.

2: Critical Thinking

Overcoming mental blocks and biases requires critical thinking skills. Critical thinking involves analyzing information objectively, evaluating its relevance and reliability, and considering multiple perspectives before drawing conclusions.

3: Open-Mindedness

Being open-minded is essential for overcoming mental blocks and biases. Open-minded individuals are willing to consider new ideas and perspectives, even if they contradict their existing beliefs or assumptions.

4: Flexibility

Flexibility in thinking is key to overcoming mental blocks and biases. Being able to adapt to new information and changing circumstances allows individuals to approach problems from different angles and consider alternative solutions.

5: Creativity

Overcoming mental blocks and biases can stimulate creativity. By breaking free from conventional thinking patterns, individuals can explore innovative ideas and approaches to problem-solving.

6: Seeking Feedback

Seeking feedback from others can help individuals overcome mental blocks and biases. Feedback provides alternative viewpoints and can highlight blind spots or biases that the individual may not be aware of.

7: Mindfulness

Practicing mindfulness can help individuals overcome mental blocks and biases by promoting awareness of their thoughts and emotions. Mindfulness techniques, such as meditation, can help individuals stay focused and calm, reducing the impact of biases on decision-making.

8: Continuous Learning

Overcoming mental blocks and biases requires a commitment to continuous learning. By staying informed about new information and developments in their field, individuals can expand their knowledge and challenge their existing beliefs.

In conclusion, overcoming mental blocks and biases is essential for effective problem-solving, particularly in complex situations. By developing critical thinking skills, maintaining an open mind, and seeking feedback from others, individuals can overcome these obstacles and approach problems with clarity and objectivity.

Chapter 3
Enhancing Analytical Thinking Skills

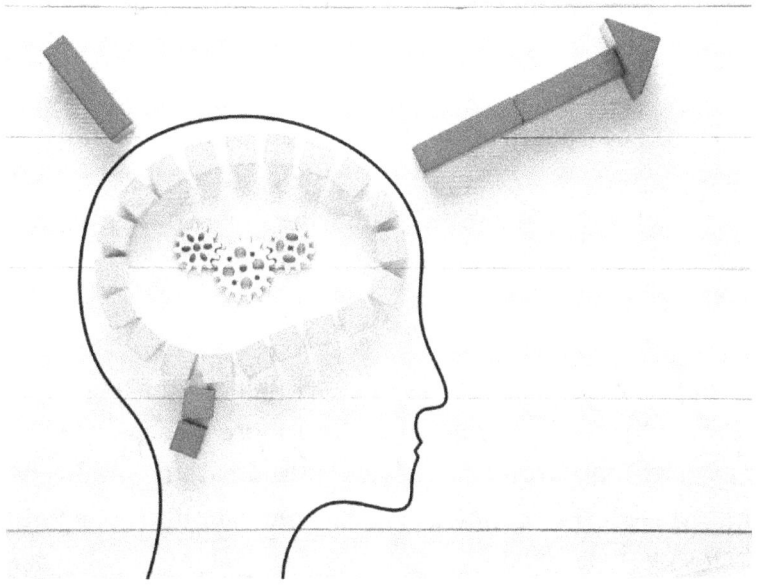

A: Breaking Down Problems into Manageable Parts

Breaking down problems into manageable parts is a fundamental step in effective problem-solving, especially when dealing with complex issues. This approach, often referred to as decomposition, involves breaking a complex problem into smaller, more manageable components. Here's a detailed exploration of how breaking down problems into manageable parts contributes to problem-solving.

1: Clarification of the Problem

Breaking down a problem helps clarify its scope and objectives. By identifying the specific aspects of the problem that need to be addressed, individuals can avoid ambiguity and focus their efforts more effectively.

2: Identification of Root Causes

Breaking down a problem allows individuals to identify its root causes. By analyzing the underlying factors contributing to the problem, individuals can develop more targeted and effective solutions.

3: Simplification of Complexity

Complex problems can be overwhelming. Breaking them down into smaller parts makes them more manageable and easier to understand. It allows individuals to tackle one aspect of the problem at a time, reducing the feeling of being overwhelmed.

4: Allocation of Resources

Breaking down a problem helps allocate resources more efficiently. By identifying the specific components of the problem that require attention, individuals can allocate resources such as time, money, and manpower more effectively.

5: Facilitation of Collaboration

Breaking down a problem can facilitate collaboration among team members. Each team member can be assigned a specific component of the problem to work on, allowing for parallel processing and faster problem resolution.

6: Development of Action Plans

Breaking down a problem helps in the development of action plans. By identifying the specific steps needed to address each component of the problem, individuals can create a roadmap for solving the problem systematically.

7: Evaluation of Progress

Breaking down a problem allows for the evaluation of progress. By tracking the completion of each component, individuals can assess how much of the problem has been solved and adjust their approach if necessary.

8: Enhancement of Problem-Solving Skills

Breaking down problems into manageable parts enhances problem-solving skills. It teaches individuals to analyze problems systematically, identify key components, and develop effective solutions.

In conclusion, breaking down problems into manageable parts is a critical step in effective problem-solving, especially when dealing with complex issues. It helps clarify the problem, identify root causes, simplify complexity, allocate resources efficiently, facilitate collaboration, develop action plans, evaluate progress, and enhance problem-solving skills.

B: Identifying Patterns and Trends

Identifying patterns and trends is a crucial aspect of problem-solving, particularly in complex situations where solutions may not be immediately apparent. By recognizing recurring patterns and trends, individuals can gain valuable insights into the underlying causes of problems and develop more effective solutions. Here's a detailed exploration of how identifying patterns and trends contributes to problem-solving:

1: Understanding the Problem

Identifying patterns and trends can help individuals understand the nature of the problem they are facing. By recognizing common patterns in data or behavior, individuals can gain a clearer picture of the problem's scope and complexity.

2: Diagnosing Root Causes

Patterns and trends can often reveal underlying root causes of problems. By analyzing data over time or across different variables, individuals can identify factors that contribute to the problem and develop targeted solutions.

3: Predicting Future Outcomes

Recognizing patterns and trends can help individuals predict future outcomes. By extrapolating from existing data, individuals can anticipate how the problem may evolve and take proactive measures to address potential challenges.

4: Optimizing Decision Making

Patterns and trends can inform decision-making processes. By identifying past trends and their outcomes, individuals can make more informed decisions about how to approach current problems and avoid past mistakes.

5: Identifying Opportunities

Patterns and trends can also reveal opportunities for improvement or innovation. By recognizing patterns that indicate areas of potential growth or development, individuals can capitalize on these opportunities to achieve positive outcomes.

6: Enhancing Problem-Solving Skills

Identifying patterns and trends enhances problem-solving skills. It teaches individuals to analyze data critically, recognize meaningful patterns, and apply these insights to develop effective solutions.

7: Facilitating Communication

Patterns and trends can facilitate communication among team members. By visually representing data trends, individuals can communicate complex information more effectively and collaborate on solutions.

8: Supporting Continuous Improvement

Identifying patterns and trends supports continuous improvement efforts. By monitoring trends over time, individuals can track the effectiveness of their solutions and make adjustments to improve outcomes.

In conclusion, identifying patterns and trends is a critical aspect of problem-solving, particularly in complex situations. It helps individuals understand the problem, diagnose root causes, predict future outcomes, optimize decision-making, identify opportunities, enhance problem-solving skills, facilitate communication, and support continuous improvement.

C: Utilizing Data and Evidence Effectively

Utilizing data and evidence effectively is essential for problem-solving, particularly in complex situations where decisions must be based on reliable information. Data and evidence can provide valuable insights into the nature of a problem, its causes, and potential solutions. Here's a detailed exploration of how utilizing data and evidence contributes to problem-solving:

1: Informing Decision Making

Data and evidence can inform decision-making processes. By analyzing relevant data, individuals can make informed decisions based on facts rather than assumptions or personal opinions.

2: Identifying Patterns and Trends

Data analysis can help individuals identify patterns and trends that may not be apparent otherwise. By analyzing data over time or across different variables, individuals can gain insights into the underlying causes of problems and develop more effective solutions.

3: Supporting Hypotheses

Data and evidence can support hypotheses about the nature of a problem and potential solutions. By collecting and analyzing data, individuals can test their hypotheses and refine their understanding of the problem.

4: Measuring Progress

Data and evidence can be used to measure progress towards solving a problem. By setting measurable goals and tracking progress over time, individuals can assess the effectiveness of their solutions and make adjustments as needed.

5: Improving Accountability

Data and evidence can improve accountability in problem-solving efforts. By documenting decisions and outcomes based on data, individuals can hold themselves and others accountable for their actions and decisions.

6: Enhancing Communication

Data and evidence can enhance communication among team members and stakeholders. By presenting data visually and clearly, individuals can communicate complex information more effectively and facilitate discussions about potential solutions.

7: Identifying Best Practices

Data and evidence can help individuals identify best practices for problem-solving. By analyzing data from past problem-solving efforts, individuals can identify strategies that have been effective in similar situations and apply them to current problems.

8: Supporting Continuous Improvement

Data and evidence support continuous improvement efforts. By analyzing data from past problem-solving efforts, individuals can identify areas for improvement and develop strategies to address them in future problem-solving efforts.

In conclusion, utilizing data and evidence effectively is essential for problem-solving, particularly in complex situations. It helps inform decision-making, identify patterns and trends, support hypotheses, measure progress, improve accountability, enhance communication, identify best practices, and support continuous improvement efforts.

Chapter 4
Embracing Systems Thinking

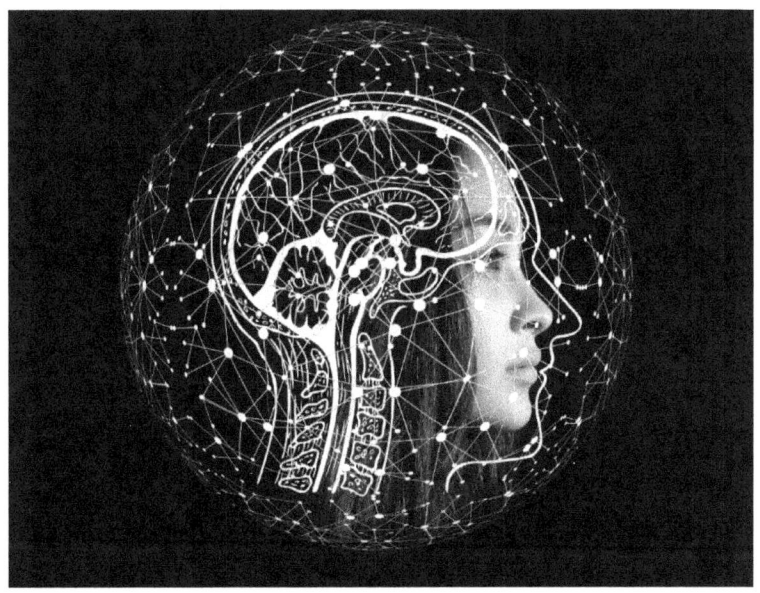

A: Understanding Interconnectedness and Interdependencies

Understanding interconnectedness and interdependencies is crucial for effective problem-solving, especially in complex situations where various factors influence each other. Interconnectedness refers to the relationships and connections between different elements, while interdependencies describe how these elements depend on each other. Here's a detailed exploration of how understanding interconnectedness and interdependencies contributes to problem-solving.

1: Holistic Perspective

Understanding interconnectedness and interdependencies allows individuals to take a holistic perspective when analyzing problems. Rather than focusing on isolated factors, individuals can consider how various elements interact and influence each other.

2: Identifying Root Causes

Interconnectedness and interdependencies can help individuals identify root causes of problems. By analyzing the relationships between different elements, individuals can pinpoint underlying factors that contribute to the problem.

3: Predicting Consequences

Understanding interconnectedness and interdependencies allows individuals to predict the consequences of their actions. By considering how changes in one element can impact others, individuals can anticipate potential outcomes and make more informed decisions.

4: Identifying Leverage Points

Interconnectedness and interdependencies reveal leverage points where small changes can lead to significant impacts. By identifying these points, individuals can focus their efforts on areas where they can have the most significant effect.

5: Avoiding Unintended Consequences

Understanding interconnectedness and interdependencies helps individuals avoid unintended consequences. By considering how changes in one element can affect others, individuals can take steps to mitigate negative impacts.

6: Facilitating Collaboration

Interconnectedness and interdependencies facilitate collaboration among team members. By understanding how their work relates to others, team members can collaborate more effectively and coordinate their efforts towards solving the problem.

7: Enhancing Systems Thinking

Understanding interconnectedness and interdependencies enhances systems thinking. Systems thinking involves considering the broader context in which a problem exists and understanding how different elements interact to form a complex system.

8: Improving Decision Making

Interconnectedness and interdependencies improve decision-making processes. By understanding the relationships between different elements, individuals can make decisions that consider the broader impact on the system as a whole.

In conclusion, understanding interconnectedness and interdependencies is essential for effective problem-solving, particularly in complex situations. It allows individuals to take a holistic perspective, identify root causes, predict consequences, identify leverage points, avoid unintended consequences, facilitate collaboration, enhance systems thinking, and improve decision-making processes.

B: Identifying Feedback Loops and System Dynamics

Identifying feedback loops and system dynamics is crucial for understanding complex systems and their behavior. Feedback loops are recurring patterns of interactions within a system that can either reinforce or dampen a change. System dynamics refer to the behavior of a system over time, influenced by feedback loops and other factors. Here's a detailed exploration of how identifying feedback loops and system dynamics contributes to problem-solving:

1: Understanding Cause-and-Effect Relationships

Feedback loops help individuals understand cause-and-effect relationships within a system. By identifying feedback loops, individuals can see how changes in one part of the system can lead to changes in other parts.

2: Predicting System Behavior

Identifying feedback loops and system dynamics allows individuals to predict how a system will behave over time. By understanding the feedback loops that drive system behavior, individuals can anticipate trends and outcomes.

3: Identifying Leverage Points

Feedback loops often have leverage points where small changes can have a significant impact on the system. By identifying these leverage points, individuals can focus their efforts on areas where they can make the most difference.

4: Avoiding Unintended Consequences

Understanding feedback loops helps individuals avoid unintended consequences. By considering how changes in one part of the system can affect other parts, individuals can take steps to mitigate negative impacts.

5: Facilitating System Optimization

Feedback loops and system dynamics can be used to optimize system performance. By identifying and strengthening positive feedback loops while dampening negative feedback loops, individuals can improve the overall functioning of the system.

6: Enhancing Systems Thinking

Identifying feedback loops and system dynamics enhances systems thinking. Systems thinking involves understanding how different elements of a system interact to produce specific outcomes.

7: Improving Decision Making

Understanding feedback loops and system dynamics improves decision-making processes. By considering the long-term effects of decisions on system behavior, individuals can make more informed choices.

8: Facilitating Continuous Improvement

Feedback loops and system dynamics facilitate continuous improvement efforts. By monitoring system behavior and adjusting strategies in response, individuals can adapt to changing circumstances and improve system performance over time.

In conclusion, identifying feedback loops and system dynamics is essential for effective problem-solving, particularly in complex systems. It helps individuals understand cause-and-effect relationships, predict system behavior, identify leverage points, avoid unintended consequences, optimize system performance, enhance systems thinking, improve decision-making processes, and facilitate continuous improvement efforts.

C: Applying Systems Thinking in Real-Life Situations

Applying systems thinking in real-life situations involves understanding how different elements interact within a system to produce specific outcomes. Systems thinking is crucial for addressing complex problems that involve multiple interconnected factors. Here's a detailed exploration of how applying systems thinking contributes to problem-solving:

1: Understanding Interconnections

Systems thinking helps individuals understand the interconnections between different elements of a system. By identifying these interconnections, individuals can see how changes in one part of the system can affect other parts.

2: Identifying Feedback Loops

Systems thinking involves identifying feedback loops within a system. These loops can either reinforce or dampen a change, leading to specific system behaviors over time.

3: Considering Time Delays

Systems thinking considers time delays in the system. Changes in one part of the system may not have immediate effects but can lead to delayed impacts in other parts of the system.

4: Recognizing System Boundaries

Systems thinking helps individuals recognize the boundaries of a system. This involves understanding which elements are part of the system being studied and which are external factors that may influence the system.

5: Holistic Problem Solving

Applying systems thinking allows for holistic problem-solving approaches. Rather than focusing on isolated factors, individuals consider the entire system and how different elements interact to produce outcomes.

6: Anticipating Unintended Consequences

Systems thinking helps individuals anticipate unintended consequences of actions. By considering the ripple effects of decisions on the entire system, individuals can take steps to mitigate negative impacts.

7: Facilitating Collaboration

Systems thinking facilitates collaboration among stakeholders. By understanding the interconnected nature of the system, stakeholders can work together to address complex problems more effectively.

8: Improving Decision Making

Applying systems thinking improves decision-making processes. By considering the broader implications of decisions on the entire system, individuals can make more informed choices.

9: Promoting Innovation

Systems thinking promotes innovation by encouraging individuals to explore new ideas and approaches. By understanding the complex interactions within a system, individuals can identify novel solutions to complex problems.

In conclusion, applying systems thinking in real-life situations is essential for effective problem-solving, particularly in complex systems. It helps individuals understand interconnections, identify feedback loops, consider time delays, recognize system boundaries, promote holistic problem-solving, anticipate unintended consequences, facilitate collaboration, improve decision making, and promote innovation.

Chapter 5
Harnessing Creativity and Innovation

A: Thinking Outside the Box

Thinking outside the box is a creative problem-solving approach that involves considering unconventional solutions and perspectives. This approach is valuable for tackling complex problems that may not have straightforward solutions. Here's a detailed exploration of how thinking outside the box contributes to problem-solving:

1: Breaking Mental Barriers

Thinking outside the box helps break mental barriers that limit creativity. By encouraging individuals to explore new ideas and perspectives, this approach expands the possibilities for problem-solving.

2: Encouraging Innovation

Thinking outside the box encourages innovation by fostering a mindset of exploration and experimentation. By considering unconventional solutions, individuals can discover new approaches that may not have been considered using traditional methods.

3: Challenging Assumptions

Thinking outside the box challenges assumptions and preconceived notions. By questioning existing beliefs about the problem, individuals can uncover hidden opportunities and novel solutions.

4: Promoting Creativity

Thinking outside the box promotes creativity by encouraging individuals to think in new and unconventional ways. This approach stimulates the imagination and can lead to innovative problem-solving strategies.

5: Exploring Multiple Perspectives

Thinking outside the box involves considering multiple perspectives and viewpoints. By looking at the problem from different angles, individuals can gain a deeper understanding of its complexity and identify creative solutions.

6: Finding Unconventional Solutions

Thinking outside the box often leads to finding unconventional solutions to problems. By thinking creatively, individuals can discover innovative approaches that may not have been obvious using traditional problem-solving methods.

7: Inspiring Others

Thinking outside the box can inspire others to think creatively as well. By modeling innovative thinking, individuals can encourage their colleagues to explore new ideas and approaches to problem-solving.

8: Adapting to Change

Thinking outside the box helps individuals adapt to change. By being open to new ideas and approaches, individuals can respond more effectively to changing circumstances and unexpected challenges.

9: Enhancing Problem-Solving Skills

Thinking outside the box enhances problem-solving skills by encouraging individuals to approach problems in new and creative ways. This approach strengthens critical thinking and analytical skills, leading to more effective problem-solving outcomes.

In conclusion, thinking outside the box is a valuable approach to problem-solving, particularly in complex situations. It breaks mental barriers, encourages innovation, challenges assumptions, promotes creativity, explores multiple perspectives, finds unconventional solutions, inspires others, adapts to change, and enhances problem-solving skills.

B: Generating and Evaluating Novel Ideas

Generating and evaluating novel ideas is a key aspect of creative problem-solving, particularly when tackling complex problems. This process involves generating a wide range of ideas and then critically evaluating them to determine their feasibility and effectiveness. Here's a detailed exploration of how generating and evaluating novel ideas contributes to problem-solving:

1: Divergent Thinking

Generating novel ideas requires divergent thinking, which involves exploring a wide range of possible solutions. By encouraging creativity and exploring unconventional ideas, individuals can generate a diverse set of options.

2: Brainstorming

Brainstorming is a common technique used to generate novel ideas. By gathering a group of individuals and encouraging them to share ideas freely, brainstorming can lead to the generation of innovative solutions.

3: Mind Mapping

Mind mapping is another technique used to generate and organize ideas. By visually representing connections between ideas, individuals can explore different possibilities and generate new insights.

4: Critical Thinking

Evaluating novel ideas requires critical thinking skills. By considering factors such as feasibility, cost, and impact, individuals can assess the potential effectiveness of each idea.

5: Prioritization

Once ideas have been generated, they must be prioritized based on their potential impact and feasibility. By prioritizing ideas, individuals can focus their efforts on implementing the most promising solutions.

6: Prototype Development

Developing prototypes or mock-ups of ideas can help evaluate their feasibility and effectiveness. By creating prototypes, individuals can test ideas in a low-risk environment and gather feedback for refinement.

7: Feedback Loop

The process of generating and evaluating novel ideas often involves a feedback loop. By gathering feedback from stakeholders and incorporating it into the ideation process, individuals can refine their ideas and improve their chances of success.

8: Risk-Taking

Generating and evaluating novel ideas often requires taking risks. By being open to failure and learning from mistakes, individuals can push the boundaries of conventional thinking and discover innovative solutions.

9: Collaboration

Generating and evaluating novel ideas is often a collaborative process. By working together with colleagues and stakeholders, individuals can benefit from diverse perspectives and insights.

In conclusion, generating and evaluating novel ideas is a critical aspect of creative problem-solving, particularly in complex situations. It involves divergent thinking, brainstorming, mind mapping, critical thinking, prioritization, prototype development, feedback loops, risk-taking, and collaboration. By employing these techniques, individuals can generate innovative solutions to complex problems.

C: Creating a Culture of Innovation

Creating a culture of innovation is essential for fostering creativity and problem-solving within an organization. Such a culture encourages employees to generate new ideas, experiment with new approaches, and embrace change. Here's a detailed exploration of how creating a culture of innovation contributes to problem-solving:

1: Encouraging Creativity

A culture of innovation encourages employees to think creatively and explore new ideas. By creating an environment that values creativity, organizations can stimulate innovative thinking and problem-solving.

2: Fostering Collaboration

Innovation often thrives in collaborative environments where ideas can be shared and developed collectively. By fostering a culture of collaboration, organizations can leverage the diverse perspectives of their employees to solve complex problems.

3: Embracing Risk-Taking

Innovation requires a willingness to take risks and try new approaches. A culture of innovation encourages employees to take calculated risks and learn from failure, fostering a mindset that is conducive to creative problem-solving.

4: Promoting Continuous Learning

Innovation is driven by a commitment to continuous learning and improvement. A culture of innovation encourages employees to seek out new knowledge and skills, which can enhance their problem-solving abilities.

5: Empowering Employees

A culture of innovation empowers employees to take ownership of their ideas and initiatives. By giving employees the freedom to experiment and innovate, organizations can tap into their full creative potential.

6: Rewarding Innovation

Recognizing and rewarding innovative ideas and efforts can reinforce a culture of innovation. By acknowledging and celebrating creativity, organizations can motivate employees to continue generating innovative solutions.

7: Adapting to Change

Innovation requires organizations to be adaptable and responsive to change. A culture of innovation encourages organizations to embrace change as an opportunity for growth and innovation.

8: Leading by Example

Creating a culture of innovation starts with leadership. Leaders who demonstrate a commitment to innovation and creativity set the tone for the entire organization, inspiring employees to embrace new ideas and approaches.

9: Creating a Supportive Environment

Finally, creating a culture of innovation requires organizations to create a supportive environment where employees feel comfortable sharing their ideas and taking risks. This includes providing access to resources, such as training and development opportunities that can help employees innovate effectively.

In conclusion, creating a culture of innovation is essential for fostering creativity and problem-solving within organizations. Such a culture encourages creativity, fosters collaboration, embraces risk-taking, promotes continuous learning, empowers employees, rewards innovation, adapts to change, leads by example, and creates a supportive environment for innovation to thrive.

Chapter 6
Utilizing Problem-Solving Tools and Techniques

A: Root Cause Analysis

Root cause analysis (RCA) is a systematic process for identifying the underlying causes of problems or issues. It aims to determine what happened, why it happened, and how to prevent it from happening again in the future. RCA is crucial for effective problem-solving, particularly in complex situations where multiple factors may contribute to a problem. Here's a detailed exploration of how root cause analysis contributes to problem-solving.

1: Identifying the Problem

The first step in RCA is to clearly define the problem or issue. This involves gathering relevant information, defining the scope of the problem, and understanding its impact.

2: Gathering Data

RCA requires collecting data related to the problem. This may include analyzing documents, interviewing stakeholders, reviewing incident reports, and examining relevant data sources.

3: Identifying Possible Causes

Once data is collected, the next step is to identify possible causes of the problem. This involves brainstorming and analyzing the data to determine what factors may have contributed to the issue.

4: Analyzing Causes

After identifying possible causes, the next step is to analyze them to determine their validity and relevance. This may involve using tools such as cause-and-effect diagrams, Pareto charts, or the 5 Whys technique to delve deeper into the root causes.

5: Determining Root Causes

The goal of RCA is to identify the root causes of the problem, not just the symptoms. Root causes are the underlying issues that, if addressed, can prevent the problem from recurring.

6: Developing Solutions

Once root causes are identified, the next step is to develop solutions to address them. These solutions should be practical, actionable, and focused on preventing the problem from happening again.

7: Implementing Solutions

After developing solutions, the next step is to implement them. This may involve making changes to processes, procedures, or systems to address the root causes of the problem.

8: Monitoring and Evaluating

Finally, after implementing solutions, it's essential to monitor their effectiveness and evaluate the results. This helps ensure that the problem has been adequately addressed and that similar issues do not occur in the future.

In conclusion, root cause analysis is a systematic process for identifying the underlying causes of problems or issues. It involves defining the problem, gathering data, identifying possible causes, analyzing causes, determining root causes, developing solutions, implementing solutions, and monitoring and evaluating results. By using RCA, organizations can effectively solve problems, prevent them from recurring, and improve their overall performance.

B: SWOT Analysis

SWOT analysis is a strategic planning tool used to identify and understand the Strengths, Weaknesses, Opportunities, and Threats related to a business or project. It is a valuable technique for analyzing the internal and external factors that can impact the success of a business or project. Here's a detailed exploration of how SWOT analysis contributes to problem-solving:

1: Strengths (S)

Strengths are internal factors that give a business or project a competitive advantage. They can include resources such as skilled personnel, strong brand reputation, proprietary technology, or financial stability. Identifying strengths helps organizations leverage their competitive advantages to address challenges and capitalize on opportunities.

2: Weaknesses (W)

Weaknesses are internal factors that hinder a business or project's performance. They can include factors such as limited resources, outdated technology, poor management, or lack of expertise. Identifying weaknesses helps organizations address areas that need improvement and minimize potential risks.

3: Opportunities (O)

Opportunities are external factors that can benefit a business or project. They can include market trends, changes in regulations, technological advancements, or new customer segments. Identifying opportunities helps organizations capitalize on external factors that can lead to growth and success.

4: Threats (T)

Threats are external factors that can negatively impact a business or project. They can include factors such as economic downturns, increased competition, changing consumer preferences, or regulatory changes. Identifying threats helps organizations anticipate and mitigate risks that could harm their operations.

5: Strategic Planning

SWOT analysis is used as a basis for strategic planning. By identifying strengths, weaknesses, opportunities, and threats, organizations can develop strategies that capitalize on their strengths, address their weaknesses, capitalize on opportunities, and mitigate threats.

6: Decision Making

SWOT analysis helps organizations make informed decisions. By providing a comprehensive overview of internal and external factors, SWOT analysis enables organizations to weigh the pros and cons of different options and choose the most appropriate course of action.

7: Risk Management

SWOT analysis helps organizations identify and mitigate risks. By identifying weaknesses and threats, organizations can take proactive measures to address these issues and minimize their impact on operations.

8: Resource Allocation

SWOT analysis helps organizations allocate resources effectively. By identifying strengths and opportunities, organizations can prioritize resource allocation to areas that will have the greatest impact on achieving their objectives.

In conclusion, SWOT analysis is a valuable tool for problem-solving and strategic planning. It helps organizations identify strengths, weaknesses, opportunities, and threats, enabling them to develop strategies that leverage their strengths, address their weaknesses, capitalize on opportunities, and mitigate threats. By using SWOT analysis, organizations can make informed decisions, manage risks, allocate resources effectively, and achieve their objectives.

C: Fishbone Diagrams

Fishbone diagrams, also known as Ishikawa diagrams or cause-and-effect diagrams, are visual tools used to identify the root causes of a problem. They are particularly useful for analyzing complex issues with multiple contributing factors. The diagram is named for its resemblance to the skeleton of a fish, with the problem statement at the head of the "fish" and the contributing factors branching off like bones. Here's a detailed exploration of how fishbone diagrams contribute to problem-solving:

1: Identifying Root Causes

Fishbone diagrams help teams systematically identify the root causes of a problem. By visually mapping out the possible causes, teams can explore different factors that may contribute to the issue.

2: Organizing Information

Fishbone diagrams help organize information in a structured manner. By categorizing factors into different branches (e.g., people, process, technology, environment), teams can systematically analyze each category to identify potential causes.

3: Encouraging Collaboration

Fishbone diagrams encourage collaboration among team members. By involving different stakeholders in the diagramming process, teams can benefit from diverse perspectives and insights.

4: Visualizing Relationships

Fishbone diagrams help visualize the relationships between different factors. By connecting factors to the main problem statement, teams can see how different elements interact and contribute to the problem.

5: Prioritizing Action

Fishbone diagrams help teams prioritize action based on the identified root causes. By focusing on addressing the root causes rather than just the symptoms, teams can develop more effective solutions.

6: Facilitating Problem-Solving Workshops

Fishbone diagrams are often used in problem-solving workshops. By engaging participants in the diagramming process, teams can foster a collaborative environment and generate creative solutions.

7: Identifying Solutions

Fishbone diagrams can help identify potential solutions to the root causes. By brainstorming possible solutions for each factor, teams can develop a comprehensive action plan.

8: Continuous Improvement

Fishbone diagrams support continuous improvement efforts. By analyzing the effectiveness of implemented solutions and updating the diagram accordingly, teams can refine their problem-solving approach over time.

In conclusion, fishbone diagrams are valuable tools for problem-solving, particularly for analyzing complex issues with multiple contributing factors. They help identify root causes, organize information, encourage collaboration, visualize relationships, prioritize action, facilitate problem-solving workshops, identify solutions, and support continuous improvement efforts. By using fishbone diagrams, teams can systematically analyze problems and develop effective solutions.

Chapter 7
Making Decisions Under Uncertainty

A: Understanding Risk and Probability

Understanding risk and probability is crucial for effective decision-making and problem-solving, particularly in complex situations where outcomes are uncertain. Risk refers to the likelihood of an event occurring and its potential impact, while probability is a measure of the likelihood of a specific outcome. Here's a detailed exploration of how understanding risk and probability contributes to problem-solving.

1: Assessing Uncertainty

Risk and probability help assess the uncertainty associated with different outcomes. By quantifying the likelihood of various outcomes, individuals can make more informed decisions about how to address potential challenges.

2: Quantifying Impact

Risk and probability help quantify the potential impact of different outcomes. By considering both the likelihood and impact of an event, individuals can prioritize their responses and allocate resources accordingly.

3: Identifying Opportunities

Understanding risk and probability can help identify opportunities for improvement or innovation. By analyzing the likelihood and impact of different scenarios, individuals can identify areas where changes can lead to positive outcomes.

4: Supporting Decision Making

Risk and probability provide a framework for decision-making. By weighing the risks and benefits of different options, individuals can make decisions that maximize potential rewards while minimizing potential risks.

5: Mitigating Risks

Understanding risk and probability helps individuals identify and mitigate risks. By implementing risk mitigation strategies, individuals can reduce the likelihood or impact of negative outcomes.

6: Optimizing Resource Allocation

Risk and probability help optimize resource allocation. By considering the likelihood and impact of different outcomes, individuals can allocate resources in a way that maximizes their effectiveness.

7: Improving Planning

Risk and probability improve planning processes. By considering potential risks and their probabilities, individuals can develop contingency plans and prepare for a range of possible outcomes.

8: Enhancing Problem-Solving Skills

Understanding risk and probability enhances problem-solving skills. It teaches individuals to analyze situations more critically, consider a range of possible outcomes, and develop strategies to address uncertainty.

In conclusion, understanding risk and probability is essential for effective decision-making and problem-solving. It helps assess uncertainty, quantify impact, identify opportunities, support decision-making, mitigate risks, optimize resource allocation, improve planning, and enhance problem-solving skills. By incorporating risk and probability into problem-solving processes, individuals can make more informed decisions and achieve better outcomes.

B: Decision Trees

Decision trees are a visual representation of decision-making processes, often used in data analysis and machine learning. They can also be used as a problem-solving tool in various fields, including business, healthcare, and finance. Decision trees help break down complex decisions into smaller, more manageable components, making it easier to understand the implications of different choices. Here's a detailed exploration of how decision trees contribute to problem-solving:

1: Visualizing Decisions

Decision trees provide a visual representation of decision-making processes, making it easier to understand the implications of different choices. By breaking down complex decisions into smaller components, decision trees help clarify the decision-making process.

2: Identifying Options

Decision trees help identify different options available at each decision point. By considering all possible choices and their potential outcomes, decision trees ensure that all relevant options are considered.

3: Evaluating Outcomes

Decision trees help evaluate the potential outcomes of different choices. By assigning probabilities to different outcomes, decision trees provide a quantitative assessment of the likely consequences of each decision.

4: Comparing Alternatives

Decision trees help compare the potential outcomes of different choices. By visually representing the consequences of each decision, decision trees facilitate a side-by-side comparison of alternatives.

5: Identifying Risks

Decision trees help identify potential risks associated with different choices. By considering the likelihood and impact of different outcomes, decision trees highlight areas where risks are most significant.

6: Optimizing Decisions

Decision trees help optimize decision-making processes. By identifying the most favorable outcomes and their probabilities, decision trees guide decision-makers toward choices that maximize benefits and minimize risks.

7: Facilitating Communication

Decision trees facilitate communication among stakeholders. By providing a visual representation of decision-making processes, decision trees help stakeholders understand the rationale behind different choices.

8: Supporting Evidence-Based Decisions

Decision trees support evidence-based decision-making. By incorporating data and probabilities into decision-making processes, decision trees ensure that decisions are based on objective information rather than subjective opinions.

In conclusion, decision trees are valuable tools for problem-solving as they help visualize decisions, identify options, evaluate outcomes, compare alternatives, identify risks, optimize decisions, facilitate communication, and support evidence-based decisions. By using decision trees, individuals and organizations can make more informed decisions and achieve better outcomes.

C: Scenario Planning

Scenario planning is a strategic planning tool used to anticipate and prepare for future uncertainties. It involves identifying a range of possible scenarios and developing strategies to address each one. Scenario planning is particularly useful for problem-solving in complex and uncertain environments. Here's a detailed exploration of how scenario planning contributes to problem-solving:

1: Anticipating Uncertainty

Scenario planning helps organizations anticipate and prepare for future uncertainties. By considering a range of possible scenarios, organizations can develop strategies to mitigate risks and capitalize on opportunities.

2: Identifying Potential Risks and Opportunities

Scenario planning helps identify potential risks and opportunities that may arise in the future. By considering a variety of scenarios, organizations can identify trends and events that may impact their operations.

3: Developing Flexible Strategies

Scenario planning helps organizations develop flexible strategies that can adapt to different future scenarios. By considering multiple possibilities, organizations can develop strategies that are robust and resilient.

4: Testing Assumptions

Scenario planning helps test assumptions about the future. By considering alternative scenarios, organizations can challenge their existing beliefs and develop a more nuanced understanding of future possibilities.

5: Enhancing Decision Making

Scenario planning enhances decision-making processes. By considering a range of scenarios, organizations can make more informed decisions that are based on a broader understanding of future possibilities.

6: Improving Risk Management

Scenario planning improves risk management practices. By identifying potential risks and developing strategies to address them, organizations can reduce the likelihood and impact of negative events.

7: Enhancing Innovation

Scenario planning enhances innovation by encouraging organizations to think creatively about future possibilities. By considering a range of scenarios, organizations can identify new opportunities for innovation.

8: Facilitating Communication

Scenario planning facilitates communication among stakeholders. By developing a shared understanding of future possibilities, organizations can align their efforts and work together towards common goals.

In conclusion, scenario planning is a valuable tool for problem-solving in complex and uncertain environments. It helps organizations anticipate uncertainty, identify risks and opportunities, develop flexible strategies, test assumptions, enhance decision-making, improve risk management, enhance innovation, and facilitate communication. By using scenario planning, organizations can prepare for the future and achieve better outcomes.

Chapter 8
Effective Communication in Problem Solving

A: Active Listening

Active listening is a communication technique that involves fully engaging with a speaker to understand their message, both verbally and non-verbally. It is a critical skill in problem-solving as it helps build rapport, gather information effectively, and ensure that all parties feel heard and understood. Here's a detailed exploration of how active listening contributes to problem-solving.

1: Building Trust and Rapport

Active listening helps build trust and rapport with others. By showing genuine interest in their perspective and demonstrating empathy, active listeners create a positive and respectful environment for problem-solving.

2: Gathering Information

Active listening allows individuals to gather information effectively. By paying close attention to the speaker's words, tone, and body language, active listeners can gather valuable insights that may not be communicated explicitly.

3: Clarifying Understanding

Active listening helps clarify understanding. By paraphrasing and summarizing the speaker's message, active listeners can ensure that they have understood the information correctly and avoid misunderstandings.

4: Identifying Needs and Concerns

Active listening helps identify the needs and concerns of others. By listening for underlying emotions and unspoken needs, active listeners can uncover issues that may not be immediately apparent.

5: Generating Solutions

Active listening facilitates the generation of solutions. By understanding the perspectives of all parties involved, active listeners can generate creative and mutually beneficial solutions to problems.

6: Resolving Conflicts

Active listening is essential for resolving conflicts. By listening to all parties involved and seeking to understand their perspectives, active listeners can find common ground and facilitate resolution.

7: Encouraging Collaboration

Active listening encourages collaboration among team members. By fostering open communication and valuing diverse perspectives, active listeners can create a collaborative problem-solving environment.

8: Empowering Others

Active listening empowers others to share their ideas and perspectives. By demonstrating respect and empathy, active listeners create a safe space for others to express themselves and contribute to the problem-solving process.

In conclusion, active listening is a critical skill for effective problem-solving. It helps build trust and rapport, gather information effectively, clarify understanding, identify needs and concerns, generate solutions, resolve conflicts, encourage collaboration, and empower others. By practicing active listening, individuals can enhance their problem-solving abilities and build stronger relationships with others.

B: Clear and Concise Communication

Clear and concise communication is essential for effective problem-solving. It involves conveying information in a straightforward manner, avoiding jargon and unnecessary details. Clear and concise communication helps ensure that messages are understood correctly and that everyone involved in the problem-solving process is on the same page. Here's a detailed exploration of how clear and concise communication contributes to problem-solving.

1: Minimizing Misunderstandings

Clear and concise communication minimizes misunderstandings. By using simple and direct language, communicators can ensure that their message is understood correctly.

2: Facilitating Decision Making

Clear and concise communication facilitates decision-making processes. By presenting information clearly and concisely, decision-makers can make informed choices based on relevant information.

3: Saving Time

Clear and concise communication saves time. By avoiding lengthy explanations and unnecessary details, communicators can convey their message more efficiently.

4: Enhancing Clarity

Clear and concise communication enhances clarity. By focusing on the key points and avoiding ambiguity, communicators can ensure that their message is easily understood.

5: Improving Problem-Solving

Clear and concise communication improves problem-solving. By presenting problems and solutions clearly, team members can collaborate more effectively to address issues.

6: Building Trust

Clear and concise communication builds trust. By being transparent and straightforward in their communication, individuals can build credibility with others.

7: Encouraging Engagement

Clear and concise communication encourages engagement. By presenting information in an accessible manner, communicators can encourage others to participate in the problem-solving process.

8: Promoting Action

Clear and concise communication promotes action. By clearly outlining the steps needed to solve a problem, communicators can motivate others to take action.

In conclusion, clear and concise communication is essential for effective problem-solving. It minimizes misunderstandings, facilitates decision-making, saves time, enhances clarity, improves problem-solving, builds trust, encourages engagement, and promotes action. By prioritizing clear and concise communication, individuals can improve their problem-solving skills and achieve better outcomes.

C: Building Trust and Rapport

Building trust and rapport is essential for effective problem-solving, as it creates a positive and collaborative environment where team members can openly communicate and work together towards common goals. Trust and rapport are built through consistent and transparent communication, mutual respect, and empathy. Here's a detailed exploration of how building trust and rapport contributes to problem-solving:

1: Open Communication

Building trust and rapport encourages open communication. Team members feel comfortable sharing their ideas, concerns, and feedback, which is essential for identifying and solving problems effectively.

2: Effective Collaboration

Trust and rapport facilitate effective collaboration. When team members trust each other, they are more willing to work together, share resources, and support one another in solving problems.

3: Conflict Resolution

Trust and rapport help in resolving conflicts. When conflicts arise, team members who trust each other are more likely to engage in constructive dialogue and find mutually acceptable solutions.

4: Increased Creativity

Building trust and rapport can lead to increased creativity. When team members feel safe to express their ideas without fear of judgment, they are more likely to come up with innovative solutions to problems.

5: Enhanced Problem-Solving Skills

Trust and rapport enhance problem-solving skills. When team members trust each other, they are more likely to collaborate effectively, consider multiple perspectives, and come up with comprehensive solutions to complex problems.

6: Improved Decision Making

Building trust and rapport improves decision-making processes. When team members trust each other's judgment, they are more likely to make decisions collaboratively, taking into account different viewpoints and potential outcomes.

7: Boosted Morale and Motivation

Trust and rapport boost morale and motivation. When team members feel valued and respected, they are more likely to be motivated to contribute their best efforts towards solving problems and achieving common goals.

8: Strengthened Relationships

Building trust and rapport strengthens relationships among team members. This not only improves teamwork in the short term but also lays the foundation for future collaboration and problem-solving efforts.

In conclusion, building trust and rapport is crucial for effective problem-solving. It encourages open communication, effective collaboration, conflict resolution, creativity, enhanced problem-solving skills, improved decision-making processes, boosted morale and motivation, and strengthened relationships. By prioritizing trust and rapport building, teams can create a supportive and positive environment where problems can be addressed efficiently and effectively.

Chapter 9
Collaborative Problem Solving

A: Team Dynamics and Roles

Team dynamics and roles play a crucial role in problem-solving, as they determine how effectively a team can work together to identify and address issues. Team dynamics refer to the way team members interact with each other, while roles define the responsibilities and expectations of each team member. Here's a detailed exploration of how team dynamics and roles contribute to problem-solving:

1: Effective Communication

Team dynamics and roles influence communication within a team. Clear roles help ensure that everyone knows their responsibilities and can communicate effectively about the problem at hand.

2: Collaboration

Team dynamics and roles impact collaboration among team members. Well-defined roles can promote collaboration by ensuring that each team member contributes their expertise to the problem-solving process.

3: Conflict Resolution

Team dynamics and roles affect how conflicts are resolved within a team. A clear understanding of roles can help prevent conflicts from arising, while effective team dynamics can facilitate constructive resolution when conflicts do occur.

4: Decision Making

Team dynamics and roles influence the decision-making process within a team. Well-defined roles can help streamline decision-making by ensuring that the right people are involved in the process.

5: Creativity

Team dynamics and roles impact the team's ability to think creatively. A supportive team dynamic can encourage members to share their ideas freely, leading to innovative problem-solving approaches.

6: Efficiency

Team dynamics and roles can impact the efficiency of the problem-solving process. Clear roles and effective team dynamics can help ensure that the team stays focused on the task at hand and avoids unnecessary delays.

7: Accountability

Team dynamics and roles help establish accountability within a team. When each team member has a clear role and understands their responsibilities, they are more likely to take ownership of their work and contribute to the team's success.

8: Adaptability

Team dynamics and roles influence how well a team can adapt to changing circumstances. A team with strong dynamics and well-defined roles is more likely to be able to adapt quickly and effectively to unexpected challenges.

In conclusion, team dynamics and roles are critical for effective problem-solving. They impact communication, collaboration, conflict resolution, decision-making, creativity, efficiency, accountability, and adaptability within a team. By understanding and managing team dynamics and roles, teams can improve their problem-solving capabilities and achieve better outcomes.

B: Conflict Resolution

Conflict resolution is the process of addressing and resolving disagreements or disputes within a team or organization. Conflict can arise from differences in opinions, values, or goals, and if not managed effectively, it can disrupt teamwork and hinder problem-solving efforts. Here's a detailed exploration of how conflict resolution contributes to problem-solving:

1: Improved Communication

Conflict resolution improves communication within a team. By addressing underlying issues and encouraging open dialogue, team members can better understand each other's perspectives and collaborate more effectively on problem-solving.

2: Enhanced Collaboration

Conflict resolution enhances collaboration among team members. By resolving conflicts in a constructive manner, team members can work together more harmoniously towards common goals.

3: Increased Creativity

Conflict resolution can increase creativity within a team. By encouraging divergent viewpoints and exploring different ideas, conflicts can lead to innovative problem-solving approaches.

4: Faster Problem Resolution

Conflict resolution leads to faster problem resolution. By addressing conflicts promptly and effectively, teams can avoid prolonged disagreements that can delay problem-solving efforts.

5: Improved Relationships

Conflict resolution improves relationships among team members. By resolving conflicts in a positive and respectful manner, team members can build trust and strengthen their working relationships.

6: Higher Team Morale

Conflict resolution boosts team morale. By addressing and resolving conflicts, teams can create a more positive and supportive work environment, leading to higher levels of motivation and engagement.

7: Better Decision Making

Conflict resolution improves decision-making processes. By considering different viewpoints and perspectives, teams can make more informed decisions that take into account a broader range of factors.

8: Reduced Stress

Conflict resolution reduces stress within a team. By addressing conflicts proactively, team members can reduce tension and improve their overall well-being.

In conclusion, conflict resolution is essential for effective problem-solving. It improves communication, enhances collaboration, increases creativity, leads to faster problem resolution, improves relationships, boosts team morale, enhances decision making, and reduces stress. By effectively managing conflict, teams can work together more effectively to address problems and achieve their goals.

C: Leveraging Diversity in Teams

Diversity in teams refers to the variety of backgrounds, experiences, and perspectives that team members bring to the table. Leveraging diversity involves recognizing and valuing these differences to enhance team performance and problem-solving. Here's a detailed exploration of how leveraging diversity in teams contributes to problem-solving:

1: Multiple Perspectives

Diversity in teams brings multiple perspectives to problem-solving. Different team members may approach problems in unique ways based on their background and experiences, leading to more innovative solutions.

2: Enhanced Creativity

Diversity fosters creativity within teams. By bringing together individuals with different viewpoints and ideas, diverse teams are more likely to generate creative solutions to complex problems.

3: Improved Decision Making

Diversity improves decision-making processes. By considering a variety of perspectives, teams can make more informed decisions that take into account a broader range of factors.

4: Increased Flexibility

Diversity increases a team's flexibility. Different team members may be more adept at handling different aspects of a problem, allowing the team to adapt more easily to changing circumstances.

5: Better Problem Solving

Diversity leads to better problem-solving outcomes. By leveraging the unique skills and perspectives of team members, diverse teams can identify and address issues more effectively.

6: Enhanced Communication

Diversity improves communication within teams. By encouraging open dialogue and the sharing of diverse viewpoints, teams can communicate more effectively and avoid misunderstandings.

7: Improved Innovation

Diversity fosters innovation within teams. By bringing together individuals with different backgrounds and experiences, diverse teams are more likely to come up with novel ideas and approaches to problem-solving.

8: Stronger Team Relationships

Diversity strengthens relationships within teams. By valuing and respecting differences, team members can build trust and collaboration, leading to stronger team dynamics.

In conclusion, leveraging diversity in teams is essential for effective problem-solving. It brings multiple perspectives, enhances creativity, improves decision-making, increases flexibility, improves problem-solving, enhances communication, fosters innovation, and strengthens team relationships. By embracing diversity and valuing the unique contributions of each team member, teams can improve their problem-solving capabilities and achieve better outcomes.

Chapter 10

Ethical Considerations in Complex Problem Solving

A: Balancing Stakeholder Interests

Balancing stakeholder interests is a critical aspect of effective problem-solving, especially in complex situations where different stakeholders have competing priorities or conflicting needs. Stakeholders can include individuals, groups, or organizations that are affected by or have a vested interest in the outcome of a problem-solving effort. Here's a detailed exploration of how balancing stakeholder interests contributes to problem-solving.

1: Identifying Stakeholders

The first step in balancing stakeholder interests is identifying all relevant stakeholders. This involves identifying who will be affected by the problem or its solution and understanding their interests, concerns, and expectations.

2: Understanding Stakeholder Needs

Balancing stakeholder interests requires understanding the needs and priorities of each stakeholder. This involves engaging with stakeholders to gather information about their concerns, objectives, and constraints.

3: Managing Expectations

Effective problem-solving involves managing stakeholder expectations. This requires setting realistic goals and timelines, and communicating openly and transparently with stakeholders about the progress of the problem-solving effort.

4: Finding Common Ground

Balancing stakeholder interests often involves finding common ground among stakeholders with competing priorities. This requires facilitating communication and negotiation to reach mutually acceptable solutions.

5: Prioritizing Stakeholder Interests

In some cases, it may be necessary to prioritize stakeholder interests based on their importance or impact. This requires careful consideration of the potential consequences of different courses of action on each stakeholder.

6: Maintaining Flexibility

Balancing stakeholder interests requires maintaining flexibility in problem-solving approaches. This may involve revisiting assumptions, exploring alternative solutions, and adapting to changing circumstances to accommodate stakeholder needs.

7: Building Consensus

Effective problem-solving often involves building consensus among stakeholders. This requires creating a shared understanding of the problem and its potential solutions, and gaining agreement on the best course of action.

8: Evaluating Outcomes

Balancing stakeholder interests requires evaluating the outcomes of problem-solving efforts to ensure that they meet the needs and expectations of stakeholders. This involves gathering feedback from stakeholders and making adjustments as necessary.

In conclusion, balancing stakeholder interests is essential for effective problem-solving. It involves identifying stakeholders, understanding their needs, managing expectations, finding common ground, prioritizing interests, maintaining flexibility, building consensus, and evaluating outcomes. By effectively balancing stakeholder interests, problem solvers can achieve better outcomes and build stronger relationships with stakeholders.

B: Transparency and Accountability

Transparency and accountability are key principles that underpin effective problem-solving processes. Transparency involves openness, communication, and the sharing of information, while accountability refers to taking responsibility for actions and decisions. Here's a detailed exploration of how transparency and accountability contribute to problem-solving:

1: Building Trust

Transparency builds trust among stakeholders. By being transparent about the problem-solving process, including goals, methods, and outcomes, stakeholders are more likely to trust the process and the individuals involved.

2: Enhancing Communication

Transparency enhances communication within teams and with external stakeholders. By sharing information openly, team members can collaborate more effectively, and stakeholders can provide valuable input and feedback.

3: Encouraging Participation

Transparency encourages stakeholder participation. When stakeholders are informed about the problem-solving process and its progress, they are more likely to engage actively and contribute their expertise and perspectives.

4: Facilitating Decision Making

Transparency facilitates decision-making processes. By providing access to relevant information, decision-makers can make more informed decisions that are based on a comprehensive understanding of the problem and its context.

5: Ensuring Fairness

Transparency ensures fairness in problem-solving processes. By being transparent about decision-making criteria and processes, individuals can feel confident that decisions are made impartially and without bias.

6: Promoting Learning

Transparency promotes learning and improvement. By openly discussing successes and failures, individuals and teams can learn from past experiences and apply these lessons to future problem-solving efforts.

7: Enhancing Accountability

Accountability ensures that individuals are held responsible for their actions and decisions. By establishing clear roles and responsibilities, and holding individuals accountable for meeting their commitments, problem-solving processes are more likely to be effective.

8: Fostering Innovation

Transparency and accountability foster innovation. By creating a culture where individuals feel empowered to take risks and try new approaches, problem-solving efforts are more likely to result in innovative solutions.

In conclusion, transparency and accountability are essential for effective problem-solving. They build trust, enhance communication, encourage participation, facilitate decision-making, ensure fairness, promote learning, enhance accountability, and foster innovation. By embracing transparency and accountability, individuals and teams can improve their problem-solving processes and achieve better outcomes.

C: Ethical Decision Making Frameworks

Ethical decision-making frameworks provide a structured approach to addressing ethical dilemmas and ensuring that decisions are made in a principled and morally responsible manner. These frameworks help individuals and organizations navigate complex ethical issues by providing guidelines for evaluating options and choosing the most ethical course of action. Here's a detailed exploration of how ethical decision-making frameworks contribute to problem-solving:

1: Identifying Ethical Issues

Ethical decision-making frameworks help identify ethical issues that may arise in problem-solving processes. By considering the potential ethical implications of different options, individuals can address these issues proactively.

2: Clarifying Values

Ethical decision-making frameworks clarify values and principles that are important to individuals and organizations. By providing a structured approach to ethical decision-making, these frameworks help ensure that decisions are aligned with core values.

3: Considering Stakeholder Perspectives

Ethical decision-making frameworks encourage individuals to consider the perspectives of all stakeholders involved in a problem-solving process. By taking into account the interests and concerns of others, individuals can make decisions that are more likely to be perceived as fair and just.

4: Weighing Options

Ethical decision-making frameworks provide a systematic way to weigh the pros and cons of different options. By considering the ethical implications of each option, individuals can choose the option that best aligns with ethical principles.

5: Promoting Accountability

Ethical decision-making frameworks promote accountability by providing a clear rationale for decisions. By documenting the ethical reasoning behind decisions, individuals and organizations can be held accountable for their actions.

6: Mitigating Risk

Ethical decision-making frameworks help mitigate ethical risks. By providing guidelines for ethical behavior, these frameworks help individuals and organizations avoid unethical conduct that could harm their reputation or lead to legal consequences.

7: Building Trust

Ethical decision-making frameworks build trust among stakeholders. By demonstrating a commitment to ethical principles, individuals and organizations can build trust with others and strengthen their relationships.

8: Enhancing Reputation

Ethical decision-making frameworks enhance reputation. By making ethical decisions consistently, individuals and organizations can build a reputation for integrity and ethical conduct.

In conclusion, ethical decision-making frameworks are essential for effective problem-solving. They help identify ethical issues, clarify values, consider stakeholder perspectives, weigh options, promote accountability, mitigate risk, build trust, and enhance reputation. By using ethical decision-making frameworks, individuals and organizations can ensure that their problem-solving efforts are conducted in a principled and morally responsible manner.

Chapter 11
Implementing Solutions and Monitoring Progress

A: Creating Action Plans

Creating action plans is a crucial step in problem-solving, as it outlines the specific steps and timelines for implementing solutions to address identified issues. Action plans help ensure that problem-solving efforts are structured, organized, and actionable. Here's a detailed exploration of how creating action plans contributes to problem-solving:

1: Clarifying Goals

Action plans clarify the goals of the problem-solving process. By clearly defining what needs to be achieved, action plans provide a clear direction for problem-solving efforts.

2: Identifying Tasks

Action plans identify the specific tasks that need to be completed to achieve the goals. By breaking down the problem-solving process into smaller, manageable tasks, action plans make it easier to track progress and ensure that nothing is overlooked.

3: Assigning Responsibilities

Action plans assign responsibilities to individuals or teams for completing specific tasks. By clearly defining who is responsible for what, action plans help ensure accountability and avoid confusion.

4: Setting Timelines

Action plans set timelines for completing tasks. By establishing deadlines for each task, action plans help keep the problem-solving process on track and ensure that progress is made in a timely manner.

5: Allocating Resources

Action plans allocate resources, such as time, money, and manpower, to complete tasks. By ensuring that resources are allocated efficiently, action plans help optimize the problem-solving process.

6: Monitoring Progress

Action plans help monitor progress towards achieving goals. By regularly reviewing the action plan and tracking progress against timelines, individuals can identify any issues or delays and take corrective action as needed.

7: Adjusting Strategies

Action plans allow for the adjustment of strategies as needed. By monitoring progress and evaluating outcomes, individuals can identify if the current approach is not working and make changes to the action plan to improve results.

8: Ensuring Consistency

Action plans ensure consistency in problem-solving efforts. By providing a structured framework for problem-solving, action plans help ensure that everyone involved is working towards the same goals using a consistent approach.

In conclusion, creating action plans is essential for effective problem-solving. It clarifies goals, identifies tasks, assigns responsibilities, sets timelines, allocates resources, monitors progress, adjusts strategies, and ensures consistency. By creating action plans, individuals and teams can effectively implement solutions to address identified issues and achieve their problem-solving goals.

B: Setting Milestones and Key Performance Indicators

Setting milestones and key performance indicators (KPIs) is essential in problem-solving as it provides a way to measure progress and ensure that goals are being achieved effectively. Milestones are specific points along the timeline of a project that represent significant achievements, while

KPIs are quantifiable measures that track the success of a project. Here's a detailed exploration of how setting milestones and KPIs contribute to problem-solving:

1: Measuring Progress

Milestones and KPIs help measure progress towards solving a problem. By setting clear milestones and KPIs, individuals and teams can track their progress and identify any areas where they are falling behind.

2: Providing Accountability

Milestones and KPIs provide accountability for problem-solving efforts. By setting specific targets and deadlines, individuals and teams are held accountable for achieving results.

3: Guiding Decision Making

Milestones and KPIs guide decision-making processes. By providing clear targets, milestones and KPIs help individuals and teams make informed decisions about how to allocate resources and adjust strategies.

4: Identifying Challenges

Milestones and KPIs help identify challenges and obstacles in problem-solving efforts. By tracking progress against milestones and KPIs, individuals and teams can identify areas where they are facing difficulties and take corrective action.

5: Improving Communication

Milestones and KPIs improve communication among team members and stakeholders. By providing a common framework for discussing progress, milestones and KPIs help ensure that everyone is on the same page.

6: Encouraging Motivation

Milestones and KPIs encourage motivation and focus. By setting achievable milestones and KPIs, individuals and teams are motivated to work towards achieving them, leading to improved problem-solving outcomes.

7: Enhancing Efficiency

Milestones and KPIs enhance efficiency in problem-solving efforts. By providing a roadmap for achieving goals, milestones and KPIs help individuals and teams work more efficiently towards solving problems.

8: Ensuring Quality

Milestones and KPIs ensure the quality of problem-solving efforts. By setting standards and benchmarks for success, milestones and KPIs help ensure that solutions meet the desired outcomes.

In conclusion, setting milestones and KPIs is essential for effective problem-solving. It helps measure progress, provide accountability, guide decision-making, identify challenges, improve communication, encourage motivation, enhance efficiency, and ensure quality. By setting clear milestones and KPIs, individuals and teams can effectively track their progress and achieve their problem-solving goals.

C: Adapting to Changing Circumstances

Adapting to changing circumstances is crucial in problem-solving, especially in complex and dynamic environments where conditions can shift rapidly. It involves being flexible, resilient, and proactive in response to new information, challenges, or opportunities that may arise during the problem-solving process. Here's a detailed exploration of how adapting to changing circumstances contributes to problem-solving:

1: Flexibility

Adapting to changing circumstances requires flexibility in approaches and strategies. By being open to new ideas and alternative solutions, individuals and teams can adjust their approach to problem-solving as needed.

2: Resilience

Adapting to changing circumstances requires resilience in the face of setbacks and challenges. By maintaining a positive attitude and persevering in the face of adversity, individuals and teams can overcome obstacles and continue to make progress towards solving a problem.

3: Proactivity

Adapting to changing circumstances requires proactivity in anticipating and responding to potential changes. By actively monitoring the environment and seeking out new information, individuals and teams can identify changes early and take proactive steps to address them.

4: Creativity

Adapting to changing circumstances often requires creativity in finding new solutions to emerging challenges. By thinking outside the box and exploring unconventional approaches, individuals and teams can find innovative ways to solve problems in dynamic environments.

5: Collaboration

Adapting to changing circumstances often requires collaboration with others. By working together and pooling resources, individuals and teams can leverage collective expertise and experience to address complex problems.

6: Learning Orientation

Adapting to changing circumstances requires a learning orientation. By being curious and seeking out new knowledge and skills, individuals and teams can continuously improve their problem-solving abilities and adapt to new challenges.

7: Decision Making

Adapting to changing circumstances requires effective decision-making skills. By weighing the pros and cons of different options and considering the potential impact of decisions, individuals and teams can make informed choices that lead to positive outcomes.

8: Communication

Adapting to changing circumstances requires effective communication. By keeping stakeholders informed and engaged, individuals and teams can ensure that everyone is on the same page and working towards common goals.

In conclusion, adapting to changing circumstances is essential for effective problem-solving. It requires flexibility, resilience, proactivity, creativity, collaboration, a learning orientation, effective decision-making, and communication. By embracing these principles, individuals and teams can navigate complex and dynamic environments successfully and achieve their problem-solving goals.

Chapter 12

Learning from Failure and Iterating Solutions

A: Embracing a Growth Mindset

Embracing a growth mindset is crucial for effective problem-solving, as it involves believing that abilities and intelligence can be developed through dedication and hard work. This mindset encourages individuals to view challenges as opportunities for growth and to persist in the face of setbacks. Here's a detailed exploration of how embracing a growth mindset contributes to problem-solving.

1: Viewing Challenges as Opportunities

Embracing a growth mindset involves viewing challenges as opportunities for learning and growth. Rather than being discouraged by obstacles, individuals with a growth mindset see them as chances to develop new skills and strategies.

2: Persistence

Embracing a growth mindset fosters persistence in problem-solving efforts. Individuals with this mindset are more likely to persevere in the face of difficulties, knowing that their efforts will lead to improvement.

3: Resilience

Embracing a growth mindset promotes resilience in the face of failure. Individuals with this mindset are more likely to bounce back from setbacks, using them as learning experiences rather than letting them deter future efforts.

4: Openness to Learning

Embracing a growth mindset involves being open to learning new things. Individuals with this mindset seek out opportunities to expand their knowledge and skills, which can lead to more effective problem-solving strategies.

5: Adaptability

Embracing a growth mindset promotes adaptability in problem-solving. Individuals with this mindset are more willing to try new approaches and adapt their strategies based on feedback and new information.

6: Positive Attitude

Embracing a growth mindset fosters a positive attitude towards challenges. Rather than being intimidated by difficult problems, individuals with this mindset approach them with enthusiasm and a belief in their ability to succeed.

7: Continuous Improvement

Embracing a growth mindset involves a commitment to continuous improvement. Individuals with this mindset are always looking for ways to enhance their skills and performance, leading to more effective problem-solving over time.

8: Collaboration

Embracing a growth mindset promotes collaboration in problem-solving efforts. Individuals with this mindset are more likely to seek out input and feedback from others, recognizing that collaboration can lead to better solutions.

In conclusion, embracing a growth mindset is essential for effective problem-solving. It involves viewing challenges as opportunities, persisting in the face of setbacks, being open to learning, adapting to new information, maintaining a positive attitude, continuously improving, and collaborating with others. By embracing these principles, individuals can enhance their problem-solving skills and achieve better outcomes in both personal and professional contexts.

B: Post-Implementation Reviews

Post-implementation reviews (PIRs) are critical in problem-solving as they provide an opportunity to evaluate the effectiveness of solutions that have been implemented and to identify lessons learned for future problem-solving efforts. PIRs help ensure that the intended outcomes of problem-solving efforts are achieved and that any issues or challenges that arise are addressed promptly. Here's a detailed exploration of how post-implementation reviews contribute to problem-solving:

1: Evaluating Effectiveness

PIRs evaluate the effectiveness of solutions that have been implemented. By comparing the actual outcomes against the intended goals, individuals and teams can determine whether the solutions have been successful in addressing the problem.

2: Identifying Success Factors

PIRs identify the success factors that contributed to the effectiveness of solutions. By recognizing what worked well, individuals and teams can replicate these factors in future problem-solving efforts.

3: Identifying Areas for Improvement

PIRs identify areas for improvement in the problem-solving process. By highlighting any shortcomings or challenges that were encountered, individuals and teams can learn from these experiences and make improvements for future efforts.

4: Documenting Lessons Learned

PIRs document lessons learned from the problem-solving process. By capturing these insights, individuals and teams can build a knowledge base of best practices and avoid repeating mistakes in future problem-solving efforts.

5: Improving Decision Making

PIRs improve decision-making processes. By analyzing the outcomes of previous decisions, individuals and teams can make more informed decisions in future problem-solving efforts.

6: Enhancing Accountability

PIRs enhance accountability for problem-solving outcomes. By reviewing the results of previous efforts, individuals and teams can be held accountable for their actions and decisions.

7: Promoting Continuous Improvement

PIRs promote continuous improvement in problem-solving processes. By regularly reviewing and reflecting on past efforts, individuals and teams can identify areas for growth and make incremental improvements over time.

8: Facilitating Organizational Learning

PIRs facilitate organizational learning. By sharing the findings of PIRs across the organization, individuals and teams can benefit from each other's experiences and improve problem-solving capabilities collectively.

In conclusion, post-implementation reviews are essential for effective problem-solving. They evaluate effectiveness, identify success factors, identify areas for improvement, document lessons learned, improve decision-making, enhance accountability, promote continuous improvement, and facilitate organizational learning. By conducting PIRs, individuals and teams can ensure that their problem-solving efforts are effective, efficient, and sustainable.

C: Continuous Improvement

Continuous improvement is a fundamental principle in problem-solving that involves continually seeking ways to enhance processes, products, or services. It is based on the belief that there is always room for improvement and that small, incremental changes can lead to significant advancements over time. Here's a detailed exploration of how continuous improvement contributes to problem-solving:

1: Iterative Approach

Continuous improvement involves an iterative approach to problem-solving. By regularly reviewing and refining processes, individuals and teams can identify areas for improvement and make incremental changes to achieve better outcomes.

2: Feedback Loop

Continuous improvement relies on feedback to identify areas for improvement. By soliciting feedback from stakeholders and monitoring performance metrics, individuals and teams can gain insights into areas that need attention.

3: Data-Driven Decision Making

Continuous improvement is based on data-driven decision-making. By collecting and analyzing data, individuals and teams can make informed decisions about which areas to focus on and which changes to implement.

4: Kaizen Philosophy

Continuous improvement is often associated with the Kaizen philosophy, which emphasizes the importance of making small, continuous changes to improve processes. By adopting this philosophy, individuals and teams can make steady progress towards solving problems.

5: Organizational Culture

Continuous improvement is supported by an organizational culture that values learning and growth. By fostering a culture that encourages innovation and experimentation, organizations can create an environment where continuous Improvement thrives.

6: Empowerment

Continuous improvement empowers individuals and teams to take ownership of the problem-solving process. By encouraging autonomy and initiative, organizations can tap into the creativity and expertise of their employees to drive improvement.

7: Benchmarking

Continuous improvement often involves benchmarking against best practices or industry standards. By comparing performance against benchmarks, individuals and teams can identify areas where they can improve.

8: Sustainability

Continuous improvement is sustainable over the long term. By making small, manageable changes, individuals and teams can avoid burnout and maintain momentum towards achieving their problem-solving goals.

In conclusion, continuous improvement is essential for effective problem-solving. It involves an iterative approach, feedback loop, data-driven decision making, Kaizen philosophy, organizational culture, empowerment, benchmarking, and sustainability. By embracing continuous improvement, individuals and organizations can enhance their problem-solving capabilities and achieve better outcomes over time.

Chapter 13

Building Resilience in Problem Solving

A: Managing Stress and Pressure

Managing stress and pressure is crucial in problem-solving, as high levels of stress can impair decision-making and hinder the ability to think clearly and creatively. Effective stress management techniques can help individuals and teams stay focused, resilient, and productive in challenging situations. Here's a detailed exploration of how managing stress and pressure contributes to problem-solving:

1: Maintaining Focus

Stress management techniques help individuals maintain focus on problem-solving tasks. By reducing distractions and staying present, individuals can better concentrate on finding solutions to complex problems.

2: Enhancing Clarity

Managing stress and pressure enhances clarity of thought. By reducing feelings of overwhelm and anxiety, individuals can think more clearly and make better decisions.

3: Promoting Creativity

Stress management techniques promote creativity in problem-solving. By reducing stress, individuals are more likely to think outside the box and consider innovative solutions to challenges.

4: Improving Decision Making

Managing stress and pressure improves decision-making processes. By reducing the impact of stress on judgment, individuals can make more rational and informed decisions.

5: Building Resilience

Stress management techniques build resilience in problem-solving. By learning how to cope with stress effectively, individuals can bounce back from setbacks and continue to pursue solutions to problems.

6: Enhancing Problem-Solving Skills

Managing stress and pressure enhances problem-solving skills. By reducing the negative impact of stress on cognitive abilities, individuals can approach problems with a clear and strategic mindset.

7: Maintaining Health and Well-being

Stress management techniques promote overall health and well-being. By reducing stress, individuals can prevent burnout and maintain physical and mental health, which are essential for effective problem-solving.

8: Improving Relationships

Managing stress and pressure improves relationships with others. By reducing stress, individuals can communicate more effectively and collaborate with others to solve problems.

In conclusion, managing stress and pressure is essential for effective problem-solving. It helps maintain focus, enhance clarity, promote creativity, improve decision-making, build resilience, enhance problem-solving skills, maintain health and well-being, and improve relationships. By implementing stress management techniques, individuals and teams can approach problem-solving with a clear and balanced mindset, leading to better outcomes.

B: Developing Emotional Intelligence

Emotional intelligence (EI) is the ability to recognize, understand, and manage our own emotions, as well as to recognize, influence, and manage the emotions of others. Developing emotional intelligence is crucial in problem-solving, as it helps individuals navigate complex interpersonal dynamics, regulate their emotions, and make sound decisions. Here's a detailed exploration of how developing emotional intelligence contributes to problem-solving:

1: Self-Awareness

Developing EI enhances self-awareness, allowing individuals to recognize their own emotions and how they affect their thoughts and behavior. This self-awareness enables individuals to manage their emotions effectively during problem-solving, leading to better decision-making.

2: Self-Regulation

EI helps individuals develop self-regulation skills, allowing them to control impulsive reactions and manage their emotions in challenging situations. This ability to regulate emotions is essential for staying focused and calm during problem-solving.

3: Empathy

Developing EI fosters empathy, enabling individuals to understand and empathize with the emotions and perspectives of others. This empathy is crucial in problem-solving, as it helps individuals navigate interpersonal conflicts and collaborate effectively with others.

4: Social Skills

EI helps individuals develop strong social skills, such as communication, conflict resolution, and leadership skills. These social skills are essential for building and maintaining relationships with others, which is critical in collaborative problem-solving efforts.

5: Conflict Resolution

Developing EI improves conflict resolution skills, enabling individuals to manage conflicts constructively and find mutually acceptable solutions. This skill is essential in addressing disagreements and finding common ground in problem-solving.

6: Decision Making

EI enhances decision-making skills, enabling individuals to make sound and rational decisions based on both logic and emotion. This balanced approach to decision-making is essential in complex problem-solving scenarios.

7: Stress Management

Developing EI improves stress management skills, allowing individuals to cope with stress and pressure more effectively. This ability to manage stress is crucial in maintaining focus and clarity during problem-solving.

8: Leadership

EI is essential for effective leadership, as it helps leaders inspire and motivate others, build strong relationships, and navigate complex interpersonal dynamics. This leadership ability is crucial in guiding teams through problem-solving processes.

In conclusion, developing emotional intelligence is essential for effective problem-solving. It enhances self-awareness, self-regulation, empathy, social skills, conflict resolution, decision-making, stress management, and leadership. By developing EI, individuals can navigate complex problem-solving scenarios with greater ease and achieve better outcomes.

C: Maintaining Motivation and Persistence

Maintaining motivation and persistence is crucial in problem-solving, as complex problems often require sustained effort and resilience to overcome. Individuals who are motivated and persistent are more likely to stay focused, overcome obstacles, and achieve their problem-solving goals. Here's a detailed exploration of how maintaining motivation and persistence contributes to problem-solving:

1: Goal Clarity

Maintaining motivation and persistence helps individuals maintain clarity about their problem-solving goals. By staying motivated, individuals are more likely to remain focused on their objectives and work towards achieving them.

2: Positive Mindset

Motivation and persistence contribute to a positive mindset, which is essential for problem-solving. A positive mindset helps individuals approach problems with optimism and resilience, enabling them to overcome challenges more effectively.

3: Resilience

Maintaining motivation and persistence fosters resilience in problem-solving. Individuals who are motivated and persistent are better able to bounce back from setbacks and continue working towards solutions.

4: Problem-Solving Strategies

Motivation and persistence help individuals develop and implement effective problem-solving strategies. By staying motivated, individuals are more likely to explore different approaches and strategies to find solutions to complex problems.

5: Adaptability

Maintaining motivation and persistence promotes adaptability in problem-solving. Individuals who are motivated and persistent are more likely to adapt their strategies and approaches based on feedback and new information.

6: Overcoming Obstacles

Motivation and persistence help individuals overcome obstacles in problem-solving. By staying motivated, individuals are more likely to persevere in the face of challenges and find creative solutions to overcome them.

7: Achieving Goals

Maintaining motivation and persistence helps individuals achieve their problem-solving goals. By staying motivated and persistent, individuals are more likely to see their efforts through to completion and achieve successful outcomes.

8: Learning and Growth

Motivation and persistence contribute to learning and growth in problem-solving. By staying motivated, individuals are more likely to learn from their experiences and apply these lessons to future problem-solving efforts.

In conclusion, maintaining motivation and persistence is essential for effective problem-solving. It helps individuals maintain goal clarity, a positive mindset, resilience, effective problem-solving strategies, adaptability, the ability to overcome obstacles, goal achievement, and learning and growth. By staying motivated and persistent, individuals can navigate complex problem-solving scenarios with determination and achieve successful outcomes.

Chapter 14
Applying Problem-Solving Skills in Different Contexts

A: Personal Problem Solving

Personal problem-solving refers to the process of identifying, analyzing, and resolving individual challenges or issues. It involves using a systematic approach to address problems that affect one's personal life, such as relationships, health, finances, or career. Here's a detailed exploration of personal problem-solving:

1: Identifying the Problem

Personal problem-solving begins with identifying the specific issue or challenge that needs to be addressed. This may involve reflecting on personal experiences, emotions, and behaviors to understand the root cause of the problem.

2: Defining Goals

Once the problem is identified, the next step is to define clear, achievable goals. These goals should outline what the desired outcome of the problem-solving process is and provide a roadmap for reaching a solution.

3: Generating Solutions

After defining goals, the next step is to generate possible solutions to the problem. This may involve brainstorming ideas, seeking advice from others, or researching potential solutions.

4: Evaluating Solutions

Once a list of potential solutions is generated, each solution should be evaluated based on its feasibility, effectiveness, and alignment with personal values and goals. This evaluation process helps identify the best course of action.

5: Implementing the Solution

After selecting a solution, the next step is to implement it. This may involve taking specific actions, making changes to behavior or habits, or seeking support from others.

6: Monitoring Progress

Throughout the problem-solving process, it is important to monitor progress towards achieving the goals. This may involve tracking changes in behavior or attitudes, seeking feedback from others, or evaluating the effectiveness of the chosen solution.

7: Adjusting as Needed

If the initial solution does not produce the desired results, it may be necessary to adjust the approach. This may involve revisiting the problem-solving process, generating new solutions, or seeking additional support or resources.

8: Reflecting on the Outcome

Once the problem is resolved, it is important to reflect on the outcome and learn from the experience. This reflection can help identify what worked well, what could be improved, and how similar problems can be addressed in the future.

In conclusion, personal problem-solving is a valuable skill that can help individuals address challenges and improve their quality of life. By using a systematic approach to identify, analyze, and resolve personal issues, individuals can become more effective problem solvers and achieve greater success in their personal lives.

B: Professional Problem Solving

Professional problem-solving refers to the process of identifying, analyzing, and resolving complex challenges or issues that arise in a professional or work-related context. It involves using a systematic approach to address problems that affect an organization, team, project, or business. Here's a detailed exploration of professional problem-solving:

1: Identifying the Problem

Professional problem-solving begins with identifying the specific issue or challenge that needs to be addressed. This may involve gathering information, conducting research, and consulting with stakeholders to understand the root cause of the problem.

2: Defining Objectives

Once the problem is identified, the next step is to define clear, measurable objectives. These objectives should outline what the desired outcome of the problem-solving process is and provide a roadmap for reaching a solution.

3: Analyzing the Situation

After defining objectives, the next step is to analyze the situation to understand the factors contributing to the problem. This may involve conducting a thorough analysis of data, processes, and systems to identify underlying issues.

4: Generating Solutions

Once the situation is analyzed, the next step is to generate possible solutions to the problem. This may involve brainstorming ideas, consulting with experts, or conducting feasibility studies to determine the best course of action.

5: Evaluating Solutions

After generating potential solutions, each solution should be evaluated based on its feasibility, cost-effectiveness, and potential impact. This evaluation process helps identify the best solution for addressing the problem.

6: Implementing the Solution

Once a solution is selected, the next step is to implement it. This may involve developing an action plan, allocating resources, and communicating the plan to stakeholders.

7: Monitoring Progress

Throughout the implementation process, it is important to monitor progress towards achieving the objectives. This may involve tracking key performance indicators, conducting regular reviews, and adjusting the plan as needed.

8: Reviewing the Outcome

Once the solution is implemented, it is important to review the outcome and assess the effectiveness of the solution. This review process can help identify what worked well, what could be improved, and how similar problems can be addressed in the future.

In conclusion, professional problem-solving is a critical skill for success in the workplace. By using a systematic approach to identify, analyze, and resolve complex challenges, professionals can improve their decision-making, enhance their problem-solving skills, and contribute to the success of their organizations.

C: Social and Global Problem Solving

Social and global problem-solving refers to the process of identifying, analyzing, and addressing complex social, environmental, and economic issues that impact communities, societies, and the world at large. It involves using a multidisciplinary approach to understand and tackle challenges such as poverty, inequality, climate change, and global health crises. Here's a detailed exploration of social and global problem-solving:

1: Identifying the Problem

Social and global problem-solving begins with identifying pressing issues that require attention. This may involve conducting research, gathering data, and consulting with experts and stakeholders to understand the root causes and impacts of the problem.

2: Understanding Context

Once the problem is identified, it is important to understand the social, cultural, economic, and political context in which it exists. This understanding helps ensure that solutions are relevant, culturally sensitive, and sustainable.

3: Engaging Stakeholders

Social and global problem-solving often requires collaboration and cooperation among diverse stakeholders, including governments, non-profit organizations, businesses, and communities. Engaging stakeholders helps ensure that solutions are inclusive and address the needs of all affected parties.

4: Analyzing Causes and Effects

After understanding the context and engaging stakeholders, the next step is to analyze the causes and effects of the problem. This analysis may involve conducting root cause analyses, impact assessments, and risk assessments to identify key drivers and potential solutions.

5: Developing Solutions

Based on the analysis, the next step is to develop potential solutions to the problem. This may involve exploring a range of approaches, from policy changes and community interventions to technological innovations and business solutions.

6: Implementing Strategies

Once solutions are developed, they must be implemented effectively. This may involve coordinating efforts among stakeholders, mobilizing resources, and monitoring progress to ensure that the strategies are being implemented as planned.

7: Monitoring and Evaluation

Throughout the implementation process, it is important to monitor progress and evaluate the effectiveness of the strategies. This may involve tracking key performance indicators, collecting feedback from stakeholders, and adjusting strategies as needed.

8: Learning and Adaptation

Social and global problem-solving is an iterative process that requires continuous learning and adaptation. By reflecting on past experiences, identifying lessons learned, and adapting strategies accordingly, practitioners can improve their problem-solving capabilities over time.

In conclusion, social and global problem-solving is a complex and challenging endeavor that requires a multidisciplinary approach, collaboration among diverse stakeholders, and a commitment to continuous learning and adaptation. By using a systematic and inclusive approach, individuals and organizations can address some of the most pressing challenges facing societies and the world today.

Chapter 15
Leveraging Technology in Problem Solving

A: Data Analytics and Machine Learning

Data analytics and machine learning are powerful tools for problem-solving, particularly in today's data-driven world. They involve the use of advanced algorithms and statistical techniques to analyze large datasets, identify patterns, and make predictions or decisions based on data. Here's a detailed exploration of how data analytics and machine learning contribute to problem-solving:

1: Data Collection and Preparation

Data analytics and machine learning begin with the collection and preparation of data. This may involve gathering data from various sources, cleaning and organizing the data, and preparing it for analysis.

2: Exploratory Data Analysis

Once the data is prepared, the next step is to conduct exploratory data analysis (EDA). EDA involves examining the data to understand its characteristics, identify trends and patterns, and detect outliers or anomalies.

3: Statistical Analysis

Data analytics and machine learning use statistical analysis techniques to uncover relationships and patterns in the data. This may involve using descriptive statistics, correlation analysis, or hypothesis testing to gain insights from the data.

4: Machine Learning Models

Machine learning models are used to make predictions or decisions based on data. These models are trained using historical data and can be used to forecast future trends, classify data into categories, or identify anomalies in the data.

5: Predictive Analytics

Predictive analytics is a key application of data analytics and machine learning. It involves using historical data to make predictions about future events or outcomes. For example, predictive analytics can be used to forecast sales, predict customer behavior, or identify potential risks.

6: Decision Support

Data analytics and machine learning can provide decision support by providing insights and recommendations based on data. For example, these tools can help businesses optimize their operations, improve customer satisfaction, or reduce costs.

7: Real-Time Monitoring

Data analytics and machine learning can be used for real-time monitoring of data streams. This is particularly useful in applications such as fraud detection, network security, and predictive maintenance, where timely action is critical.

8: Continuous Improvement

Data analytics and machine learning can be used for continuous improvement by analyzing the results of past decisions and using this information to refine future decisions. This iterative process helps organizations improve their problem-solving capabilities over time.

In conclusion, data analytics and machine learning are powerful tools for problem-solving that can help organizations uncover insights, make informed decisions, and improve their operations. By leveraging these tools effectively, organizations can gain a competitive advantage and achieve better outcomes in a wide range of applications.

B: Simulation and Modeling

Simulation and modeling are powerful problem-solving techniques that involve creating simplified representations of complex systems to study their behavior and make predictions. These techniques are widely used in fields such as engineering, science, economics, and social sciences to understand complex phenomena and test hypotheses. Here's a detailed exploration of how simulation and modeling contribute to problem-solving:

1: Understanding Complex Systems

Simulation and modeling help in understanding complex systems by breaking them down into simpler components and studying their interactions. This allows researchers to gain insights into the underlying dynamics of the system.

2: Predictive Analysis

Simulation and modeling can be used for predictive analysis, allowing researchers to forecast the behavior of a system under different conditions. This is particularly useful for making informed decisions and planning for the future.

3: Optimization

Simulation and modeling can be used for optimization, helping researchers find the best possible solution to a problem. This is done by testing different scenarios and identifying the one that leads to the optimal outcome.

4: Risk Analysis

Simulation and modeling can be used for risk analysis, allowing researchers to assess the potential risks associated with different courses of action. This is particularly useful for mitigating risks and making informed decisions in uncertain environments.

5: Design and Planning

Simulation and modeling can be used for design and planning purposes, allowing researchers to test different design concepts and scenarios before implementing them in the real world. This can help save time and resources and avoid costly mistakes.

6: Policy Evaluation

Simulation and modeling can be used for evaluating policies and interventions, allowing researchers to assess their potential impact and effectiveness. This is particularly useful for policymakers and decision-makers in designing and implementing effective policies.

7: Training and Education

Simulation and modeling can be used for training and education purposes, allowing students and professionals to gain hands-on experience in a safe and controlled environment. This can help improve learning outcomes and enhance skills development.

8: Continuous Improvement

Simulation and modeling can be used for continuous improvement by iteratively refining models based on new data and insights. This iterative process helps researchers improve the accuracy and reliability of their models over time.

In conclusion, simulation and modeling are powerful problem-solving techniques that can help researchers gain insights into complex systems, make informed decisions, and improve outcomes in a wide range of applications. By leveraging these techniques effectively, researchers can address some of the most challenging problems facing society today.

C: Collaborative Tools and Platforms

Collaborative tools and platforms are technologies that facilitate communication, cooperation, and coordination among individuals and teams working together on a shared goal or project. These tools are essential for problem-solving in today's interconnected and globalized world, enabling teams to collaborate effectively regardless of their location. Here's a detailed exploration of how collaborative tools and platforms contribute to problem-solving:

1: Communication

Collaborative tools and platforms facilitate communication among team members, allowing them to share information, ideas, and updates in real-time. This helps teams stay connected and informed, enhancing collaboration and problem-solving.

2: Project Management

Collaborative tools and platforms provide project management features, such as task assignment, progress tracking, and deadline management. These features help teams stay organized and focused, ensuring that problem-solving efforts are efficient and effective.

3: Document Sharing and Collaboration

Collaborative tools and platforms enable teams to share and collaborate on documents, such as reports, presentations, and spreadsheets. This allows team members to work together in real-time, making it easier to gather input, make revisions, and finalize documents.

4: Virtual Meetings and Conferencing

Collaborative tools and platforms support virtual meetings and conferencing, allowing team members to meet and collaborate regardless of their location. This is particularly useful for distributed teams or teams working remotely, enabling them to maintain regular communication and collaboration.

5: Task Automation

Collaborative tools and platforms often include features for task automation, such as workflow automation and integration with other tools and systems. This helps streamline processes and reduce manual work, allowing teams to focus on problem-solving.

6: Data Security

Collaborative tools and platforms provide data security features, such as encryption and access controls, to protect sensitive information. This ensures that confidential data is protected during collaboration and problem-solving activities.

7: Version Control

Collaborative tools and platforms offer version control features, allowing teams to track and manage changes to documents and files. This helps prevent confusion and ensures that team members are working with the most up-to-date information.

8: Feedback and Evaluation

Collaborative tools and platforms enable teams to provide feedback and evaluate their progress. This helps teams identify areas for improvement and make adjustments to their problem-solving strategies.

In conclusion, collaborative tools and platforms are essential for effective problem-solving in today's fast-paced and interconnected world. By enabling communication, collaboration, and coordination among team members, these tools help teams work together more efficiently and achieve better outcomes.

Chapter 16
Future Trends in Complex Problem Solving

A: Artificial Intelligence and Automation

Artificial intelligence (AI) and automation are revolutionizing problem-solving by enabling machines to perform tasks that traditionally require human intelligence. These technologies are increasingly being used across various industries to streamline processes, enhance decision-making, and improve efficiency. Here's a detailed exploration of how AI and automation contribute to problem-solving.

1: Data Analysis

AI and automation can analyze large volumes of data quickly and accurately, uncovering insights and patterns that may not be apparent to human analysts. This is particularly useful for identifying trends, making predictions, and informing decision-making.

2: Decision Support

AI systems can provide decision support by analyzing data and recommending courses of action based on predefined criteria. This helps decision-makers make informed decisions more quickly and efficiently.

3: Process Automation

Automation can streamline repetitive tasks and processes, such as data entry, scheduling, and reporting. This frees up human resources to focus on more complex and strategic problem-solving activities.

4: Predictive Maintenance

AI and automation can be used for predictive maintenance, where machines analyze data from sensors to predict when maintenance is needed. This helps prevent costly equipment failures and downtime.

5: Natural Language Processing

AI technologies such as natural language processing (NLP) can understand and generate human language, enabling more natural and intuitive interactions between humans and machines. This is particularly useful for applications such as chatbots and virtual assistants.

6: Image and Video Analysis

AI can analyze images and videos to extract useful information, such as identifying objects, people, or patterns. This is useful in a variety of applications, from medical imaging to security surveillance.

7: Optimization

AI and automation can optimize processes and workflows by analyzing data and identifying areas for improvement. This helps organizations operate more efficiently and effectively.

8: Personalization

AI can personalize experiences for users by analyzing their behavior and preferences. This is useful in marketing, e-commerce, and other applications where tailored experiences can improve customer satisfaction and engagement.

In conclusion, AI and automation are transforming problem-solving by enabling machines to perform tasks that were once thought to be exclusive to humans. By harnessing the power of these technologies, organizations can improve efficiency, enhance decision-making, and achieve better outcomes across a wide range of industries and applications.

B: Global Challenges and Opportunities

Global challenges and opportunities refer to the complex issues and possibilities that affect the world as a whole, transcending national boundaries and requiring collective action. These challenges and opportunities span a wide range of areas, including economics, environment, health, security, and technology. Here's a detailed exploration of how addressing global challenges and opportunities contributes to problem-solving:

1: Climate Change

Climate change is one of the most pressing global challenges of our time, with far-reaching impacts on the environment, economy, and society. Addressing climate change requires collaborative efforts to reduce greenhouse gas emissions, adapt to changing climate conditions, and transition to a sustainable, low-carbon economy.

2: Poverty and Inequality

Poverty and inequality are pervasive global issues that affect millions of people around the world. Addressing poverty and inequality requires strategies that promote inclusive economic growth, improve access to education and healthcare, and reduce disparities in income and wealth.

3: Global Health

Global health challenges, such as infectious diseases, pandemics, and non-communicable diseases, require coordinated efforts to prevent, detect, and respond to health threats. This includes investing in healthcare systems, promoting vaccination, and improving access to essential medicines and treatments.

4: Food Security

Ensuring food security for a growing global population is a major challenge that requires sustainable agricultural practices, improved access to nutritious food, and efforts to reduce food waste and loss.

5: Digital Divide

The digital divide refers to the gap between those who have access to digital technologies and those who do not. Bridging the digital divide requires efforts to expand access to affordable internet connectivity, digital devices, and digital literacy programs.

6: Migration and Refugees

Addressing the challenges posed by migration and refugees requires coordinated efforts to protect the rights of migrants and refugees, address the root causes of forced displacement, and promote social cohesion and integration.

7: Technological Innovation

Technological innovation presents both challenges and opportunities, such as the potential for economic growth, job creation, and improved quality of life. However, it also raises concerns about data privacy, cyber security, and ethical use of emerging technologies.

8: Global Governance

Strengthening global governance mechanisms is essential for addressing global challenges and opportunities effectively. This includes promoting multilateral cooperation, upholding international law, and enhancing the role of international organizations.

In conclusion, addressing global challenges and opportunities requires collaborative, multidisciplinary approaches that transcend national boundaries. By working together, the international community can tackle some of the most pressing issues facing the world today and create a more sustainable and inclusive future for all.

C: The Role of Education in Developing Problem-Solving Skills

Education plays a crucial role in developing problem-solving skills, as it provides individuals with the knowledge, tools, and mindset needed to tackle complex challenges effectively. Here's a detailed exploration of how education contributes to the development of problem-solving skills:

1: Critical Thinking

Education fosters critical thinking skills, which are essential for identifying, analyzing, and evaluating problems. Critical thinking enables individuals to question assumptions, consider multiple perspectives, and make informed decisions.

2: Creativity

Education encourages creativity, which is essential for generating innovative solutions to problems. Creative thinking allows individuals to think outside the box, explore new ideas, and come up with novel approaches to solving problems.

3: Analytical Skills

Education develops analytical skills, which are crucial for breaking down complex problems into manageable parts. Analytical thinking enables individuals to identify patterns, trends, and relationships in data, which can inform problem-solving strategies.

4: Collaboration

Education promotes collaboration skills, which are essential for working effectively with others to solve problems. Collaboration involves communication, teamwork, and the ability to share ideas and feedback constructively.

5: Adaptability

Education teaches adaptability, which is important for responding to changing circumstances and unexpected challenges. Adaptability enables individuals to adjust their problem-solving strategies based on new information and feedback.

6: Persistence

Education instills a sense of persistence, which is crucial for overcoming obstacles and setbacks in problem-solving. Persistence involves perseverance, resilience, and the willingness to keep trying until a solution is found.

7: Decision Making

Education improves decision-making skills, which are essential for making informed and effective choices. Education teaches individuals how to weigh options, consider consequences, and choose the best course of action in problem-solving.

8: Lifelong Learning

Education promotes lifelong learning, which is essential for continuously improving problem-solving skills. Lifelong learning involves seeking new knowledge, acquiring new skills, and adapting to new challenges throughout life.

In conclusion, education plays a vital role in developing problem-solving skills by fostering critical thinking, creativity, analytical skills, collaboration, adaptability, persistence, decision-making, and lifelong learning. By providing individuals with the tools and mindset needed to tackle complex challenges, education prepares them to succeed in a rapidly changing world.

Chapter 17
Case Studies in Complex Problem Solving

A: Healthcare

Healthcare is a critical area where effective problem-solving can have a profound impact on individuals, communities, and society as a whole. From improving access to healthcare services to developing innovative treatments and technologies, healthcare problem-solving plays a crucial role in promoting health and well-being. Here's a detailed exploration of how problem-solving is applied in healthcare.

1: Diagnosis and Treatment

Problem-solving is central to the process of diagnosing and treating medical conditions. Healthcare professionals use problem-solving skills to analyze symptoms, interpret test results, and develop treatment plans that are tailored to individual patient needs.

2: Healthcare Delivery

Problem-solving is essential for improving the delivery of healthcare services. Healthcare administrators and policymakers use problem-solving skills to address challenges such as resource allocation, patient flow, and quality improvement.

3: Patient Safety

Problem-solving is critical for ensuring patient safety in healthcare settings. Healthcare professionals use problem-solving skills to identify and mitigate risks, prevent medical errors, and improve the overall quality of care.

4: Public Health

Problem-solving is key to addressing public health challenges, such as infectious diseases, chronic illnesses, and environmental health hazards. Public health professionals use problem-solving skills to develop and implement interventions that promote health and prevent disease.

5: Health Information Technology

Problem-solving is essential for developing and implementing health information technology (HIT) solutions. HIT professionals use problem-solving skills to design electronic health records, develop health informatics systems, and ensure the secure exchange of health information.

6: Medical Research

Problem-solving is fundamental to medical research, where researchers use problem-solving skills to design studies, analyze data, and draw meaningful conclusions. Medical research advances our understanding of disease mechanisms and leads to the development of new treatments and interventions.

7: Healthcare Innovation

Problem-solving drives innovation in healthcare, leading to the development of new medical devices, drugs, and treatment modalities. Healthcare innovators use problem-solving skills to identify unmet needs, develop novel solutions, and bring new products to market.

8: Healthcare Policy

Problem-solving is crucial for shaping healthcare policy at the local, national, and global levels. Policymakers use problem-solving skills to analyze healthcare systems, identify areas for improvement, and implement reforms that enhance access, quality, and affordability of care.

In conclusion, problem-solving is a cornerstone of healthcare, driving improvements in diagnosis, treatment, healthcare delivery, patient safety, public health, health information technology, medical research, healthcare innovation, and healthcare policy. By applying problem-solving skills to healthcare challenges, individuals and organizations can improve health outcomes, enhance patient experiences, and advance the overall quality of healthcare delivery.

B: Environmental Sustainability

Environmental sustainability is a pressing global challenge that requires effective problem-solving to address issues such as climate change, pollution, deforestation, and loss of biodiversity. Problem-solving in environmental sustainability involves identifying the root causes of environmental problems, developing innovative solutions, and implementing strategies to promote sustainable practices. Here's a detailed exploration of how problem-solving is applied in environmental sustainability:

1: Identifying Environmental Issues

Problem-solving in environmental sustainability begins with identifying key environmental issues and their underlying causes. This may involve conducting research, gathering data, and analyzing trends to understand the scope and impact of environmental problems.

2: Analyzing Environmental Impact

Problem-solving in environmental sustainability requires analyzing the environmental impact of human activities, such as greenhouse gas emissions, water pollution, and habitat destruction. This analysis helps prioritize areas for intervention and guide decision-making.

3: Developing Sustainable Practices

Problem-solving in environmental sustainability involves developing sustainable practices that minimize negative environmental impact. This may include promoting renewable energy, reducing waste, conserving water, and adopting eco-friendly technologies.

4: Implementing Conservation Strategies

Problem-solving in environmental sustainability includes implementing conservation strategies to protect natural resources and biodiversity. This may involve establishing protected areas, restoring ecosystems, and promoting sustainable land use practices.

5: Addressing Climate Change

Problem-solving in environmental sustainability requires addressing climate change through mitigation and adaptation strategies. This may include reducing carbon emissions, transitioning to clean energy sources, and building resilience to climate impacts.

6: Promoting Circular Economy

Problem-solving in environmental sustainability involves promoting a circular economy that reduces waste and promotes resource efficiency. This includes recycling, reusing, and repurposing materials to minimize environmental impact.

7: Engaging Stakeholders

Problem-solving in environmental sustainability requires engaging stakeholders, including governments, businesses, communities, and individuals. This may involve raising awareness, building partnerships, and mobilizing resources to support sustainable practices.

8: Monitoring and Evaluation

Problem-solving in environmental sustainability involves monitoring and evaluating the effectiveness of interventions. This helps ensure that efforts to promote environmental sustainability are achieving their intended goals and making a positive impact.

In conclusion, problem-solving in environmental sustainability is essential for addressing global environmental challenges and promoting a more sustainable future. By applying problem-solving skills to environmental issues, individuals and organizations can contribute to protecting the planet and ensuring a healthy environment for future generations.

C: Economic Development

Economic development refers to the sustained, concerted actions of policymakers and communities that promote the standard of living and economic health of a specific area. It involves various strategies, policies, and practices aimed at improving the economic well-being and quality of life for a community. Problem-solving in economic development is crucial for addressing challenges such as poverty, unemployment, and inequality, and for fostering sustainable economic growth. Here's a detailed exploration of how problem-solving is applied in economic development.

1: Identifying Economic Challenges

Problem-solving in economic development begins with identifying key economic challenges facing a community or region. This may include high unemployment rates, lack of access to basic services, or limited economic opportunities.

2: Analyzing Economic Trends

Problem-solving in economic development requires analyzing economic trends and data to understand the underlying causes of economic challenges. This analysis helps identify potential solutions and strategies for addressing them.

3: Developing Economic Policies

Problem-solving in economic development involves developing and implementing economic policies that promote growth and development. This may include policies to attract investment, support small businesses, and improve infrastructure.

4: Promoting Entrepreneurship

Problem-solving in economic development includes promoting entrepreneurship and innovation as drivers of economic growth. This may involve providing support and resources to aspiring entrepreneurs and fostering a culture of innovation.

5: Investing in Education and Skills Development

Problem-solving in economic development requires investing in education and skills development to ensure that the workforce is equipped with the skills needed for a modern economy. This may include vocational training, adult education programs, and initiatives to improve literacy rates.

6: Infrastructure Development

Problem-solving in economic development involves investing in infrastructure, such as transportation, energy, and telecommunications, to support economic growth. This may include building new infrastructure, upgrading existing infrastructure, and improving connectivity.

7: Supporting Small and Medium-sized Enterprises (SMEs)

Problem-solving in economic development includes supporting SMEs, which are often the backbone of the economy. This may involve providing access to finance, business development services, and market opportunities for SMEs.

8: Monitoring and Evaluation

Problem-solving in economic development requires monitoring and evaluating the impact of economic policies and programs. This helps ensure that efforts to promote economic development are effective and achieving their intended goals.

In conclusion, problem-solving in economic development is essential for addressing economic challenges, fostering sustainable economic growth, and improving the quality of life for communities. By applying problem-solving skills to economic issues, policymakers and communities can create a more prosperous and inclusive economy for all.

Chapter 18
Cultivating a Culture of Continuous Learning

A: Lifelong Learning Strategies

Lifelong learning is the process of continuously learning and developing new skills and knowledge throughout one's life. Lifelong learning is essential for personal and professional growth, as well as for adapting to an ever-changing world. Here's a detailed exploration of lifelong learning strategies:

1: Set Learning Goals

Start by setting clear and achievable learning goals. This could be acquiring a new skill, gaining knowledge in a specific area, or improving existing skills.

2: Create a Learning Plan

Develop a learning plan that outlines how you will achieve your learning goals. This could include identifying resources, setting a timeline, and breaking down your goals into smaller, manageable tasks.

3: Utilize Multiple Learning Resources

Take advantage of a variety of learning resources, such as books, online courses, workshops, and seminars. This allows you to gain different perspectives and approaches to learning.

4: Practice Regularly

Practice is key to mastering new skills. Set aside regular time for practice and repetition to reinforce your learning.

5: Seek Feedback

Feedback is essential for learning and improvement. Seek feedback from peers, mentors, or instructors to help you identify areas for improvement and refine your skills.

6: Reflect on Your Learning

Take time to reflect on your learning experiences. This could involve journaling, discussing with others, or simply thinking about what you have learned and how you can apply it.

7: Stay Curious

Cultivate a curious mindset and a desire to learn. Stay open to new ideas and experiences, and seek out opportunities for learning in everyday life.

8: Embrace Challenges

Challenges and setbacks are a natural part of the learning process. Embrace them as opportunities for growth and learning, rather than obstacles.

9: Network and Collaborate

Learning is often more effective when done in collaboration with others. Network with like-minded individuals, join study groups, or participate in online forums to enhance your learning experience.

10: Stay Updated

Keep yourself updated with the latest trends and developments in your field of interest. This could involve reading industry publications, attending conferences, or taking advanced courses.

11: Balance Depth and Breadth

While it's important to specialize and develop expertise in a specific area, it's also valuable to have a broad range of knowledge and skills. Strive for a balance between depth and breadth in your learning.

12: Celebrate Your Achievements

Celebrate your learning achievements, no matter how small. This can help motivate you to continue learning and growing.

In conclusion, lifelong learning is a valuable habit that can enhance your personal and professional life. By adopting these strategies, you can cultivate a lifelong learning mindset and continuously improve your skills and knowledge throughout your life.

B: Knowledge Sharing and Mentorship

Knowledge sharing and mentorship are valuable strategies for lifelong learning and professional development. They involve sharing knowledge, skills, and experiences with others, as well as learning from the expertise of others. Here's a detailed exploration of knowledge sharing and mentorship strategies.

1: Establish a Learning Network

Build a network of colleagues, mentors, and experts in your field who can provide valuable insights and guidance. This network can help you stay updated with industry trends and best practices.

2: Participate in Communities of Practice

Join communities of practice related to your field or interests. These communities provide opportunities to share knowledge, seek advice, and collaborate with others who share similar interests.

3: Attend Workshops and Conferences

Attend workshops, conferences, and seminars to learn from experts and peers in your field. These events provide valuable networking opportunities and expose you to new ideas and perspectives.

4: Engage in Peer Learning

Participate in peer learning activities, such as study groups or learning circles, where you can share knowledge and learn from others in a collaborative environment.

5: Seek Mentorship

Find a mentor who can provide guidance, advice, and support as you navigate your career. A mentor can offer valuable insights, help you set goals, and provide feedback on your progress.

6: Be a Mentor

Share your knowledge and experience with others by serving as a mentor. Mentoring provides an opportunity to give back to the community and help others develop their skills and achieve their goals.

7: Document and Share Best Practices

Document best practices, lessons learned, and success stories from your experiences. Sharing these insights with others can help them learn from your experiences and avoid common pitfalls.

8: Encourage a Culture of Learning

Foster a culture of learning in your organization or community by encouraging knowledge sharing, collaboration, and continuous improvement. This can be done through initiatives such as lunch-and-learn sessions, knowledge sharing platforms, or recognition programs.

9: Embrace Feedback

Be open to receiving feedback from others, as it can provide valuable insights into areas for improvement and growth. Use feedback as an opportunity to learn and develop new skills.

10: Reflect on Your Experiences

Take time to reflect on your experiences and learning journey. Reflective practice can help you gain insights into your strengths and weaknesses, as well as identify areas for further development.

In conclusion, knowledge sharing and mentorship are powerful strategies for lifelong learning and professional development. By actively participating in these activities, you can enhance your skills, expand your knowledge, and achieve your personal and professional goals.

C: Building Learning Organizations

Building a learning organization involves creating a culture and infrastructure that supports continuous learning, innovation, and adaptation. Learning organizations are able to thrive in complex and changing environments by encouraging employees to continuously develop their skills and knowledge. Here's a detailed exploration of how to build learning organizations:

1: Promote a Growth Mindset

Foster a culture that values learning and growth. Encourage employees to adopt a growth mindset, believing that their abilities can be developed through dedication and hard work.

2: Provide Learning Opportunities

Offer a variety of learning opportunities, such as training programs, workshops, seminars, and conferences. Provide access to resources, such as books, online courses, and learning platforms.

3: Encourage Experimentation

Create a safe environment where employees feel comfortable taking risks and trying new things. Encourage experimentation and learning from failure.

4: Support Knowledge Sharing

Encourage employees to share their knowledge and experiences with others. Provide platforms and tools for sharing information, such as intranet portals, collaboration tools, and knowledge management systems.

5: Empower Employees

Empower employees to take ownership of their learning and development. Encourage them to set learning goals and provide support and resources to help them achieve those goals.

6: Lead by Example

Leaders play a crucial role in building learning organizations. Lead by example and demonstrate a commitment to learning and development. Encourage openness, curiosity, and a willingness to learn from others.

7: Reward Learning and Innovation

Recognize and reward employees who demonstrate a commitment to learning and innovation. This could include promotions, bonuses, or other forms of recognition.

8: Create Learning Communities

Foster a sense of community among employees by creating learning groups or communities of practice. Encourage collaboration and knowledge sharing among employees with similar interests or goals.

9: Measure and Evaluate Learning

Monitor and evaluate the effectiveness of learning initiatives. Collect feedback from employees and stakeholders to identify areas for improvement and make adjustments as needed.

10: Adapt to Change

Be flexible and adaptable in response to changing circumstances. Encourage employees to embrace change as an opportunity for learning and growth.

By building a learning organization, you can create a culture that values continuous learning and innovation, ultimately leading to improved performance, employee satisfaction, and organizational success.

Chapter 19
The Role of Leadership in Complex Problem Solving

A: Vision and Strategic Planning

Vision and strategic planning are essential components of organizational success, providing a roadmap for achieving goals and guiding decision-making. They involve setting a clear vision for the future and developing strategies to achieve that vision. Here's a detailed exploration of vision and strategic planning.

1: Vision Setting

Vision setting involves defining a compelling and inspiring vision for the organization's future. This vision should align with the organization's values and mission and provide a clear direction for growth and development.

2: Environmental Analysis

Strategic planning begins with an analysis of the external environment, including market trends, competitor analysis, and regulatory changes. This analysis helps identify opportunities and threats that may impact the organization's strategic direction.

3: Internal Assessment

Strategic planning also involves an assessment of the organization's internal capabilities, including strengths, weaknesses, resources, and competencies. This assessment helps identify areas where the organization can leverage its strengths and address its weaknesses.

4: Setting Strategic Goals

Based on the vision and environmental analysis, strategic goals are set to guide the organization's efforts. These goals should be specific, measurable, achievable, relevant, and time-bound (SMART) to ensure they are effective.

5: Developing Strategies

Strategies are developed to achieve the strategic goals set by the organization. These strategies outline the actions and initiatives that will be taken to move the organization towards its vision. Strategies may include market expansion, product development, or process improvement initiatives.

6: Resource Allocation

Strategic planning involves allocating resources, such as budget, personnel, and time, to support the implementation of the strategies. This requires prioritizing initiatives based on their importance and potential impact on the organization's goals.

7: Monitoring and Evaluation

Strategic planning is an ongoing process that requires monitoring and evaluation to ensure that goals are being met and strategies are effective. This involves tracking key performance indicators (KPIs) and making adjustments to the plan as needed.

8: Communication and Engagement

Effective strategic planning requires communication and engagement with stakeholders, including employees, customers, and partners. This helps ensure alignment and buy-in for the strategic direction of the organization.

9: Adaptation to Change

Strategic planning should be flexible and adaptable to changes in the external environment. This may require revisiting the vision and strategies to ensure they remain relevant and effective in a changing world.

10: Continuous Improvement

Strategic planning should be a continuous process of learning and improvement. Organizations should regularly review their strategies and performance to identify areas for improvement and make adjustments to achieve their vision.

In conclusion, vision and strategic planning are essential for organizational success, providing a roadmap for achieving goals and guiding decision-making. By setting a clear vision, conducting thorough environmental and internal assessments, setting strategic goals, developing effective strategies, allocating resources, monitoring and evaluating progress, communicating effectively, and adapting to change, organizations can create a path to success and achieve their long-term objectives.

B: Empowering Teams and Individuals

Empowering teams and individuals is essential for creating a culture of trust, collaboration, and innovation within an organization. It involves providing individuals with the autonomy, resources, and support they need to take ownership of their work and contribute to the organization's goals. Here's a detailed exploration of how to empower teams and individuals:

1: Provide Clear Goals and Expectations

Clearly define goals, expectations, and responsibilities to give teams and individuals a clear understanding of what is expected of them. This helps align efforts towards common objectives.

2: Delegate Authority

Delegate authority to teams and individuals to make decisions and take action within their areas of responsibility. This allows them to take ownership of their work and be accountable for the outcomes.

3: Encourage Initiative and Innovation

Encourage teams and individuals to take initiative and think innovatively. Provide opportunities for them to propose new ideas, experiment with new approaches, and contribute to continuous improvement.

4: Offer Training and Development

Provide training and development opportunities to help teams and individuals develop new skills, expand their knowledge, and grow professionally. This enhances their capabilities and empowers them to take on new challenges.

5: Provide Resources and Support

Provide teams and individuals with the resources, tools, and support they need to succeed. This includes access to information, technology, training, and mentoring.

6: Foster a Collaborative Environment

Create a collaborative environment where teams and individuals feel comfortable sharing ideas, seeking feedback, and working together towards common goals. This encourages teamwork and mutual support.

7: Recognize and Reward Achievement

Recognize and reward teams and individuals for their achievements and contributions. This can be done through formal recognition programs, rewards, or simply acknowledging their efforts and accomplishments.

8: Promote Work-Life Balance

Encourage work-life balance by offering flexible work arrangements, promoting wellness initiatives, and respecting employees' personal time. This helps prevent burnout and promotes overall well-being.

9: Provide Regular Feedback

Provide regular feedback to teams and individuals on their performance, progress towards goals, and areas for improvement. This helps them stay on track and continuously improve.

10: Lead by Example

Leaders play a crucial role in empowering teams and individuals. Lead by example by demonstrating trust, transparency, and open communication. Show appreciation for their efforts and encourage a culture of empowerment throughout the organization.

In conclusion, empowering teams and individuals is essential for fostering a culture of engagement, creativity, and productivity within an organization. By providing clear goals and expectations, delegating authority, encouraging initiative and innovation, offering training and development, providing resources and support, fostering a collaborative environment, recognizing and rewarding achievement, promoting work-life balance, providing regular feedback, and leading by example, organizations can empower their teams and individuals to achieve their full potential and drive success.

C: Leading by Example

Leading by example is a powerful leadership approach that involves setting a positive example through actions, behaviors, and decisions. It is about demonstrating the values, behaviors, and work ethic that you want to see in others. Here's a detailed exploration of leading by example:

1: Demonstrating Integrity

Leaders who lead by example demonstrate integrity in their actions and decisions. They are honest, ethical, and consistent in their behavior, earning the trust and respect of their team.

2: Showing Respect

Leaders show respect for others by listening attentively, valuing diverse perspectives, and treating everyone with dignity and respect. They create a positive and inclusive work environment.

3: Being Accountable

Leaders take responsibility for their actions and decisions. They admit mistakes, learn from them, and strive to do better in the future. This sets a precedent for accountability within the team.

4: Communicating Effectively

Leaders communicate clearly, openly, and transparently. They keep their team informed, listen to feedback, and address concerns promptly. This promotes trust and understanding within the team.

5: Demonstrating Commitment

Leaders demonstrate commitment to the organization's goals and values. They are dedicated to their work, show enthusiasm, and inspire others to do their best.

6: Showing Empathy

Leaders show empathy towards their team members, understanding their needs, concerns, and challenges. They provide support and encouragement, creating a positive and supportive work environment.

7: Promoting Collaboration

Leaders promote collaboration and teamwork by encouraging cooperation, sharing information, and fostering a sense of unity among team members. They lead by example by collaborating with others and seeking input from team members.

8: Encouraging Growth

Leaders encourage personal and professional growth among team members. They provide opportunities for learning and development, mentorship, and career advancement.

9: Adapting to Change

Leaders demonstrate flexibility and adaptability in the face of change. They embrace new ideas, technologies, and ways of working, inspiring their team to do the same.

10: Celebrating Success

Leaders celebrate success and recognize the achievements of their team. They show appreciation for hard work and dedication, motivating team members to continue striving for excellence.

In conclusion, leading by example is a powerful leadership approach that can inspire and motivate others to perform at their best. By demonstrating integrity, showing respect, being accountable, communicating effectively, demonstrating commitment, showing empathy, promoting collaboration, encouraging growth, adapting to change, and celebrating success, leaders can create a positive and productive work environment where teams thrive and succeed.

Chapter 20

Conclusion

Becoming a Master Problem Solver

In conclusion, mastering complex problem-solving is a valuable skill that can greatly benefit your personal and professional life. It requires a combination of analytical thinking, creativity, effective communication, and collaboration. By developing a problem-solving mindset, utilizing the right tools and techniques, and continuously learning and adapting, you can become a master problem solver in any situation.

A: Developing a Problem-Solving Mindset

Developing a problem-solving mindset is foundational to becoming a master problem solver. It involves cultivating a set of attitudes and behaviors that enable you to approach challenges with confidence and creativity. Here's a detailed exploration of how to develop a problem-solving mindset:

1: Be Curious

Curiosity is essential for problem-solving. Be curious about the world around you, ask questions, and seek to understand how things work. Curiosity drives exploration and discovery, leading to innovative solutions.

2: Embrace Challenges

Instead of avoiding challenges, embrace them as opportunities for growth and learning. Challenges stretch your abilities and help you develop new skills and insights.

3: Stay Positive

Maintain a positive attitude even in the face of setbacks and challenges. A positive mindset helps you stay motivated and focused on finding solutions rather than dwelling on problems.

4: Be Open-Minded

Approach problems with an open mind, willing to consider different perspectives and possibilities. Being open-minded allows you to see things from different angles and come up with creative solutions.

5: Think Critically

Develop your critical thinking skills by analyzing information, evaluating arguments, and making informed decisions. Critical thinking helps you identify underlying issues and find effective solutions.

6: Seek Feedback

Be open to feedback from others, as it can provide valuable insights and perspectives that you may not have considered. Feedback helps you improve your problem-solving skills and refine your approaches.

7: Collaborate with Others

Problem-solving is often a collaborative effort. Collaborate with others to leverage their expertise and insights, and to come up with innovative solutions together.

8: Be Resilient

Develop resilience to overcome challenges and setbacks. Resilience helps you bounce back from failures and setbacks, and stay focused on finding solutions.

9: Practice Creative Thinking

Cultivate your creativity by exploring new ideas, experimenting with different approaches, and thinking outside the box. Creativity is essential for generating innovative solutions to complex problems.

10: Continuously Learn and Grow

Adopt a growth mindset that sees challenges as opportunities for learning and growth. Continuously seek to expand your knowledge and skills, and apply them to solving problems in new and creative ways.

In conclusion, developing a problem-solving mindset is essential for becoming a master problem solver. By being curious, embracing challenges, staying positive, being open-minded, thinking critically, seeking feedback, collaborating with others, being resilient, practicing creative thinking, and continuously learning and growing, you can develop the mindset needed to tackle even the most complex problems effectively.

B: Utilizing the Right Tools and Techniques

Mastering complex problem-solving requires more than just a mindset—it also involves using the right tools and techniques to analyze, understand, and address problems effectively. Here's a detailed exploration of some key tools and techniques:

1: SWOT Analysis

SWOT analysis is a framework used to identify and analyze the strengths, weaknesses, opportunities, and threats related to a specific situation or problem. It helps organizations understand their current position and make informed decisions about future strategies.

2: Root Cause Analysis

Root cause analysis is a method used to identify the underlying causes of a problem. By digging deep into the root causes, rather than just addressing symptoms, organizations can develop more effective solutions that prevent the problem from recurring.

3: Scenario Planning

Scenario planning is a strategic planning technique that involves creating multiple scenarios or possible futures based on different assumptions. This helps organizations anticipate and prepare for future challenges and opportunities.

4: Data Analytics

Data analytics involves using data to analyze trends, patterns, and relationships to gain insights and inform decision-making. This can include techniques such as data mining, predictive analytics, and machine learning.

5: Technology Tools

Technology tools such as project management software, collaboration platforms, and data visualization tools can help streamline the problem-solving process and improve communication and collaboration among team members.

6: Decision Trees

Decision trees are a visual representation of decision-making processes, showing the possible outcomes of different decisions and the probabilities associated with each outcome. They can help organizations make informed decisions based on data and analysis.

7: Fishbone Diagrams (Ishikawa or Cause-and-Effect Diagrams)

Fishbone diagrams are used to identify and analyze the possible causes of a problem. They help teams brainstorm and organize potential causes into categories, making it easier to identify root causes.

8: Risk Analysis

Risk analysis involves identifying, assessing, and prioritizing risks associated with a project or decision. It helps organizations understand the potential impact of risks and develop strategies to mitigate them.

9: Benchmarking

Benchmarking involves comparing your organization's performance or practices to those of other organizations to identify best practices and areas for improvement. It can help organizations learn from others and improve their problem-solving approaches.

10: Process Mapping

Process mapping involves visually representing a process to identify inefficiencies, bottlenecks, and areas for improvement. It helps organizations streamline processes and improve overall efficiency.

In conclusion, mastering complex problem-solving involves using the right tools and techniques to analyze, understand, and address problems effectively. By leveraging frameworks such as SWOT analysis, root cause analysis, and scenario planning, as well as technology and data analytics, organizations can develop more effective solutions and make informed decisions that drive success.

C: Continuous Learning and Adaptation

Problem-solving is not a one-time activity but a dynamic process that requires continuous learning and adaptation. To become a master problem solver, you must embrace a mindset of lifelong learning and be open to acquiring new knowledge, skills, and perspectives. Here's a detailed exploration of how continuous learning and adaptation contribute to mastering complex problem-solving:

1: Staying Curious

Curiosity is the foundation of continuous learning. By staying curious and asking questions, you can uncover new information, insights, and perspectives that can help you better understand and solve problems.

2: Seeking New Knowledge and Skills

The world is constantly evolving, and so are the problems we face. To stay ahead, you must actively seek out new knowledge and skills that are relevant to your field. This may involve taking courses, attending workshops, or reading books and articles.

3: Being Open to Feedback

Feedback is essential for growth and improvement. Be open to receiving feedback from others, whether it's from colleagues, mentors, or customers. Use feedback as an opportunity to learn from your mistakes and refine your problem-solving approach.

4: Embracing Change

The ability to adapt to change is crucial for problem-solving. Be flexible and open-minded when faced with new challenges or unexpected obstacles. Look for creative solutions and be willing to try new approaches.

5: Reflecting on Past Experiences

Take time to reflect on past problem-solving experiences. What worked well? What could have been done differently? Reflecting on past experiences can help you identify patterns and improve your problem-solving skills.

6: Experimenting with New Ideas

Don't be afraid to try new ideas and approaches. Experimentation is key to innovation and can lead to breakthrough solutions. Be willing to take calculated risks and learn from both successes and failures.

7: Networking and Collaboration

Learning doesn't happen in isolation. Build a strong network of colleagues, mentors, and experts who can provide support, advice, and new perspectives. Collaboration can lead to innovative solutions that may not have been possible alone.

8: Adopting a Growth Mindset

A growth mindset is the belief that abilities can be developed through dedication and hard work. Adopting a growth mindset can help you overcome challenges and persist in the face of setbacks, ultimately leading to greater success in problem-solving.

In conclusion, continuous learning and adaptation are essential for mastering complex problem-solving. By staying curious, seeking new knowledge and skills, being open to feedback and change, and embracing a growth mindset, you can continuously improve your problem-solving abilities and achieve greater success in both your personal and professional life.

D: Effective Communication and Collaboration

Effective communication and collaboration are essential components of problem-solving, particularly in complex and team-oriented environments. They involve conveying ideas clearly, listening actively, and working together cohesively to find innovative solutions. Here's a detailed exploration of how effective communication and collaboration contribute to mastering complex problem-solving:

1: Clear Communication

Clear communication is crucial for ensuring that ideas, information, and expectations are conveyed accurately. It involves using language that is easy to understand, providing context when necessary, and being concise yet comprehensive in your communication.

2: Active Listening

Active listening is a key component of effective communication. It involves fully concentrating on what is being said, understanding the message, and responding thoughtfully. Active listening helps build rapport, understand different perspectives, and avoid misunderstandings.

3: Open and Honest Communication

Open and honest communication fosters trust and transparency within teams. It involves sharing information openly, expressing opinions respectfully, and addressing conflicts or issues directly. Open communication encourages collaboration and innovation.

4: Feedback and Reflection

Providing and receiving feedback is essential for continuous improvement. Effective feedback is specific, constructive, and focused on behaviors or actions. Reflecting on feedback helps individuals and teams learn from their experiences and improve their problem-solving skills.

5: Empathy and Emotional Intelligence

Understanding the emotions and perspectives of others is crucial for effective collaboration. Empathy involves putting yourself in someone else's shoes and recognizing their feelings and needs. Emotional intelligence helps manage emotions and navigate interpersonal dynamics effectively.

6: Flexibility and Adaptability

Effective communication and collaboration require flexibility and adaptability. This involves being open to different ideas and approaches, willing to compromise when necessary, and adjusting your communication style to suit the needs of the situation or team.

7: Setting Clear Goals and Roles

Clearly defining goals, objectives, and roles within a team helps ensure that everyone is on the same page. This clarity enables team members to work together more effectively towards a common objective.

8: Utilizing Technology and Tools

Technology and collaboration tools can facilitate communication and collaboration, especially in remote or distributed teams. Tools such as project management software, video conferencing, and messaging platforms can help teams stay connected and organized.

9: Resolving Conflicts

Conflict is inevitable in any team environment, but how it is managed can impact problem-solving efforts. Effective conflict resolution involves addressing conflicts calmly and constructively, focusing on finding solutions rather than placing blame.

10: Celebrating Achievements

Recognizing and celebrating achievements, both big and small, helps boost morale and motivation within a team. It also reinforces a culture of collaboration and teamwork.

In conclusion, effective communication and collaboration are essential for mastering complex problem-solving. By communicating clearly, listening actively, collaborating effectively, and fostering a positive and supportive team environment, individuals and teams can overcome challenges, find innovative solutions, and achieve success.

E: Creativity and Innovation

Creativity and innovation are crucial components of mastering complex problem-solving. They involve thinking creatively, generating new ideas, and approaching problems from new angles. Here's a detailed exploration of how creativity and innovation contribute to problem-solving:

1: Thinking Outside the Box

Creativity involves thinking outside the box and exploring unconventional solutions. It requires breaking away from traditional thinking patterns and exploring new possibilities.

2: Generating Novel Ideas

Innovation is about generating novel ideas and solutions to problems. This may involve brainstorming, mind mapping, or other creative techniques to generate a wide range of ideas.

3: Evaluating Ideas

Not all ideas will be feasible or effective. Evaluating ideas involves critically assessing their potential impact, feasibility, and alignment with goals before deciding which ones to pursue.

4: Experimenting and Iterating

Innovation often involves experimentation and iteration. It's important to test ideas, gather feedback, and make adjustments based on results to improve their effectiveness.

5: Creating a Culture of Innovation

Fostering a culture of innovation within your team or organization is essential for encouraging creativity and innovation. This involves promoting a mindset that values experimentation, learning from failure, and continuous improvement.

6: Encouraging Diverse Perspectives

Creativity thrives in diverse environments. Encouraging diverse perspectives and experiences within your team can lead to more innovative solutions by bringing different viewpoints to the table.

7: Providing Resources and Support

Creativity requires resources and support. Providing access to tools, technology, and training can help individuals and teams unleash their creative potential.

8: Embracing Risk-Taking

Innovation involves taking risks and being willing to try new things. Encouraging a culture that embraces calculated risk-taking can lead to breakthrough solutions.

9: Rewarding Innovation

Recognizing and rewarding innovation can motivate individuals and teams to continue thinking creatively and pushing boundaries.

10: Continuous Learning and Improvement

Creativity and innovation require continuous learning and improvement. Encouraging individuals and teams to learn from their experiences and adapt their approaches can lead to ongoing innovation.

In conclusion, creativity and innovation are essential for mastering complex problem-solving. By thinking creatively, generating novel ideas, experimenting, and creating a culture that values innovation, individuals and teams can tackle even the most challenging problems and find innovative solutions.

Read More Interested Book!

www.ingramcontent.com/pod-product-compliance
Lightning Source LLC
Chambersburg PA
CBHW050059230526
45470CB00004B/1590